A PERCH IN BOHEMIA

A PERCH IN BOHEMIA

Art, love and life in Chelsea's Swan Court
1931-1961

*To Barbara
with best wishes
for your birthday,
Nicola*

Nicola Braban

Copyright © 2020 Nicola Braban

Cover design: Jim Sutherland
Linocut: Rebecca Sutherland

The moral right of the author has been asserted.

Apart from any fair dealing for the purposes of research or private study, or criticism or review, as permitted under the Copyright, Designs and Patents Act 1988, this publication may only be reproduced, stored or transmitted, in any form or by any means, with the prior permission in writing of the publishers, or in the case of reprographic reproduction in accordance with the terms of licences issued by the Copyright Licensing Agency. Enquiries concerning reproduction outside those terms should be sent to the publishers.

Matador
9 Priory Business Park,
Wistow Road, Kibworth Beauchamp,
Leicestershire. LE8 0RX
Tel: 0116 279 2299
Email: books@troubador.co.uk
Web: www.troubador.co.uk/matador
Twitter: @matadorbooks

ISBN 978 1838594 244

British Library Cataloguing in Publication Data.
A catalogue record for this book is available from the British Library.

Printed and bound by CPI Group (UK) Ltd, Croydon, CR0 4YY
Typeset in 12pt Adobe Jenson Pro by Troubador Publishing Ltd, Leicester, UK

Matador is an imprint of Troubador Publishing Ltd

*To all the residents of Swan Court,
past, present and future*

'The charm of history and its enigmatic lesson is that, from age to age, nothing changes and yet everything is different.'

ALDOUS HUXLEY
A REGULAR VISITOR TO SWAN COURT IN THE 1930S

Contents

	Preface	ix
1.	Building Swan Court 1929-1931	1
2.	The First Residents and their World	8
3.	The Blue Plaque Couple: Edward McKnight Kauffer and Marion Dorn	24
4.	The Artists' Friend: Eric Craven (Peter) Gregory	39
5.	The Photographer and his Muse: Francis Bruguière and Rosalinde Fuller	45
6.	A Double Life: Antony Gibbons Grinling	60
7.	The Broken-Hearted Poet: The Hon. Bryan Guinness	69
8.	An Occasional Modernist: Francis Lorne	79
9.	The Unlikely Couple: Ernest Milton and Naomi Royde-Smith	85
10.	The Saucy Ingénue: Nancy O'Neil	96
11.	Wooing Chaplin's Girl: Virginia Cherrill and the Earl of Jersey	100
12.	Actors and Activists: Theatre's Golden Couple: Dame Sybil Thorndike and Sir Lewis Casson	113
13.	A Risky Affair: Captain Peter and Mrs Dorothy Eckersley	125

14.	A Controversial Historian: Sir Arthur Bryant	143
15.	The Mitford Boy: The Hon. Thomas Freeman-Mitford	154
16.	The Passionate Bibliophile: John Hayward	159
17.	On the Wilder Shores: Lesley Blanch	172
18.	The *Picture Post* Pair: Anne Scott-James and Macdonald Hastings	185
19.	Crime's Queen and her Consort: Dame Agatha Christie and Sir Max Mallowan	197
20.	The Newly-Weds: Denis and Margaret Thatcher	208
	Postscript	220
	Acknowledgements	222
	Bibliography	223

Preface

If you turn off the King's Road in Chelsea by the Old Town Hall and head down Chelsea Manor Street, you can't help but notice Swan Court. A handsome rather forbidding red-brick building, it dominates the streetscape on your left, its eight storeys towering over the huddled roofs of Chelsea Manor Studios and blocking the afternoon sun from the terraced houses of Flood Street on the other side. It must have seemed a modern upstart in 1931 when its decorated brickwork erupted into the post-war Chelsea landscape, cocking a snook at the neo-classicism of the Town Hall and the jumble of workshops, studios and eighteenth-century cottages that crowded round its skirts.

I've known the building all my adult life, paying my first visit as a teenager to a girlfriend who briefly lived in one of the maisonettes. We spent the long summer day with the windows shut, playing Chubby Checker on her Dansette record player and practising the Twist. A hundred yards away the sixties were swinging in the King's Road, and to our teenage selves Swan Court seemed more than a touch out of date. Yet when the block had first opened its doors thirty years before, it was dashingly modern, its uncluttered labour-saving spaces offering a new way of living to Londoners in flight from the over-stuffed opulence of Edwardian mansion flats. The building's mix of maisonettes, flats and artists' studios was appealing, and renting was easy. With long leases nearly four decades in the future, tenants perched for a few months or years, swapping flats and moving in and out as the mood took them.

In the nineteen-thirties the building was home to an eclectic mix of people, retired army officers and war widows rubbing shoulders with a clutch of hopeful artists and newly emancipated single girls. In among them I found a rather different group, creative, colourful, racy, now moving into their middle years. Often friends as well as neighbours, their lives intertwined at home, at work and in the salons and streets of Chelsea, in a web of artistic, literary and political interests. Some became, and have remained, well-known. Others have slipped into the shadows.

As I began to explore their lives, I was struck by how vividly the most significant preoccupations of Britain in the nineteen-thirties were exemplified in this group of people who happened for a short space of time to live under the same roof. Modernist art, architecture and design, the marriage of art and commerce, political disillusion and the search for meaning in the aftermath of the Great War, the lure of Fascism and admiration for Germany, the joys of free love, the thrill of new technology and the national passions for radio, cinema and sea-travel… all were to be found within these individual stories, living witness to the innovations and obsessions of an extraordinary decade.

By the end of the war only three of this early group remained, the others gone, along with much of the connected Chelsea world that had nurtured them. And as the new generation embraced rock-and-roll and brutalist architecture in the sixties, the last remnants of Swan Court's pre-war brush with modernity vanished.

Neither honours, celebrity nor length of residence played any part in my choice of subjects, although some attained all three. Dame Sybil Thorndike, much celebrated in her day, honoured, and resident for over thirty years, has a place alongside John Hayward, an intriguing and largely forgotten character, resident for just a few months. In particular I looked for people like Hayward, whose story would illuminate some corner of a long-vanished world, for original talents like Edward McKnight Kauffer, Marion Dorn and Francis Bruguière, for controversial characters like Arthur Bryant and Dorothy Eckersley, or bold eccentrics like Rosalinde Fuller and Lesley Blanch. The eighteen biographical essays that resulted are snap-shots of the life and work of a remarkable group of true individuals.

Nicola Braban
February 2020

Swan Court from Chelsea Manor Street. The Architects' Journal, October 7th 1931.

I
Building Swan Court
1929-1931

Anyone wanting a snapshot of Chelsea's social and architectural mix in the late nineteen-twenties only had to take a stroll down the King's Road. Starting from Sloane Square, you passed mansion flats, art galleries and antique shops interspersed with dairies, food shops and cafés. Studios, from the grand to the ramshackle, dotted the side streets. Painters, poets and their muses strolled the pavements and drank in the pubs beside a road increasingly filled with expensive motor cars. By the time you reached the Bluebird Garage on the corner of The Vale, with its parking spaces for three hundred cars and its segregated lounges for owners, ladies and chauffeurs, you were almost at the limit of artistic Chelsea. A step or two further on, around the bend in the road, and you were in an area known to locals as the World's End. Starting from the World's End pub and extending for three hundred yards either side of the King's Road, streets of mouldering terraces sprinkled with small factories crouched in the shadow of the Lots Road power station. These two Chelseas, just yards apart and within one of London's richest boroughs, were visibly and psychologically separate entities, most of the social interaction involving the women of the World's End who came in their dozens into the 'other' Chelsea each day to work as domestic cleaners.

The World's End was the most notorious example of run-down housing in Chelsea, but it was not the only one; away from the King's Road, pockets of painted cottages rubbed shoulders with shabby lodging-houses, workshops and warrens of cheap studios. Then, towards the end of the twenties, land prices began to rise, starting a boom that lasted throughout the next decade and brought swathes of dilapidated buildings under the bulldozer to make way for new middle-class housing. The World's End itself survived intact until the war, when its industry attracted the attentions of the Luftwaffe.

By the end of the thirties, a series of huge apartment blocks dominated the Chelsea skyline. The first to go up was Swan Court in 1931, followed by Sloane Avenue Mansions in 1933. Cranmer Court, then one of the largest blocks in London, was built between 1934 and 1935. Nell Gwynne House and the vast ten storeys of Chelsea Cloisters had appeared by 1938. Several of these blocks had underground parking, and some – including Swan Court from 1937 – had restaurants open to the public. The borough's new architecture was a curious mixture of the gigantic looming blocks with terraces of neo-Georgian houses. Hardly cutting-edge stuff, although those with a fancy for something more adventurous took heart when two Modernist houses appeared in Old Church Street – No 64 by Eric Mendelson and Serge Chermayeff, and No 66 by Walter Gropius and Maxwell Fry – bringing a little whiff of Continental avant-garde to the streets of Chelsea.

The ground on which Swan Court was to rise can be seen on a 1920 Cadogan Estate plan which shows two plots numbered 4 and 7 running between Flood Street and Manor Street (now Chelsea Manor Street) and extending from Chelsea Manor Studios to Wellington Street (now Flood Walk). From 1927, the jumble of workshops on the two plots was leased by Wolseley Motors, who moved out in March 1929 after being taken over by Morris. The licence to assign the remaining Wolseley lease was granted to Ben Allsop, a chartered surveyor who'd marked down the land as ideal for the building of flats. Cadogan retained the freehold which it holds to this day.

Allsop was a man of entrepreneurial streak who had founded his firm, Allsop & Co, in 1906. After returning from the war, he opened an office in Soho Square and rapidly made his mark as an expert advisor to property developers keen to build the now fashionable blocks of smaller serviced flats. Allsop was a key figure in the planning and building of Swan Court, and the managing agent from its inception until his retirement. A keen Territorial soldier, it may well have been his influence that led to Swan Court being home in its early years to many serving and retired officers and war widows. Perhaps he had a hand too in the letting, in 1939, of flat 27 to the newly formed 97th Anti-Aircraft Brigade.

According to his obituary, Allsop was much concerned about the plight of unmarried mothers, so was surely in sympathy with Lady Violet Melchett's charitable efforts in the building that arose on the other half of the plot next door to Swan Court. A campaigner over the years for infant welfare and the Chelsea Health Society, Violet Melchett had long wanted to develop a health centre in the area, and her husband, the industrialist and politician Baron Melchett, was keen to indulge her passion. Previously Sir Alfred Mond, he'd made a fortune out of chemical engineering, culminating in the creation of Imperial Chemical Industries (ICI) whose state-of-the art chemical plant in north-east England so impressed the writer Aldous Huxley that he immortalised Sir Alfred as the character Mustapha Mond, Resident World Controller of Western Europe, in his novel *Brave New World*, which was published in 1931 just before Swan Court opened.

In 1929, Mond – now Lord Melchett – bought the lease of the whole Cadogan site for £14,000, keeping a plot for the Health Centre before selling the remainder to a newly-formed development company to build the flats that were to become Swan Court.

When it came to choosing architects, Melchett's eye fell on a Birmingham-based practice, Buckland and Hayward, who landed the job of designing both the Violet Melchett Centre and Swan Court. The firm was reputable, but the choice was not entirely based on merit: the Melchetts' daughter Rosalind was married at the time to Herbert Buckland's son Francis, also a partner in the practice. Although the Health Centre and the flats were not in any way connected, the choice of the same architects was a happy one for the streetscape, the two buildings generally seen as comfortably compatible. An excellent example to the planners of future high-rise buildings in the area, said *The Times*' architectural correspondent.

Buckland and Hayward planned the eight floors of Swan Court in a quadrangle around a central courtyard, with arched entrances giving access to Manor Street (now

Chelsea Manor Street) on the west side and Flood Street to the east. The central part of the two street façades was deeply recessed to form a projecting block at each corner, allowing for a forecourt on both streets. Reviews in the architectural press were enthusiastic: the *Architects' Journal* praised the arched heads of the main entrances, the porches and the window boxes, the use of rusticated bricks for the quoins and the 'pleasant plum colour' of the bricks. Inside, the architects opted for some cautiously Art Deco features in cornices, door design and lettering, while going to town in the two lobbies with modern lighting, green walls, red and gold cornices and terrazzo floors painted with a white swan design.

Swan Court's main claim to originality lay in the unusual mix of accommodation, which the architects saw as appropriate to an artistic quarter such as Chelsea. With one hundred and four flats of varying sizes, plus twenty-four

'Comfortably compatible'. Swan Court with the Violet Melchett Mothercraft Centre in the foreground, October 1931. The Architects' Journal, *October 7th 1931.*

maisonettes and sixteen eighth-floor studios, the building was designed to appeal to artists and single people as well as families. The maisonettes, combining the attractions of a house with the practical advantages of a flat, were believed to be unique in London. All the flats were economical to run and labour-saving, with built-in cupboards and kitchens with refrigerators and larders. Electric light and power and constant hot water were laid on. Rents were attractive – between £160 and £250 per annum inclusive of rates and taxes and with no extra charges. The flats were devoid of decorative features, the rooms plain, well-proportioned boxes on which individual tenants could impose their own taste.

This was not luxury, but for many people, the prospect of life with modern conveniences, minimal paid help and a contemporary twist was appealing. The flats were popular from the start, with the first advertisement appearing in *The Times* on July 21st 1931 and running monthly till the following

One of the two entrance lobbies, with modern lighting, green walls and red and gold cornices. The Architects' Journal, October 7th 1931.

summer, when only a few remained unlet. This was no bold experiment in living, like Wells Coates' 1934 Lawn Road Flats in Belsize Park, but it acknowledged and catered for a significant shift in attitudes towards domestic life amongst a growing band of middle-income Londoners.

MAIN SOURCES

Architecture Illustrated November 1931: 'Flat 144 interiors' pp.143,144
Burke, David: *The Lawn Road Flats: Spies, Writers and Artists*. Boydell, 2014.
Royal Institute of British Architects (RIBA) archive.
The Times, March 26th 1931: 'Violet Melchett Centre Opening by the Queen'.
The Architect and Building News, March 27th 1931: 'The Violet Melchett Infant Welfare Centre, Chelsea' p.143.
The Architect's Journal, October 7th 1931: 'Flats with Artists' Studios' p.465
Wheal, Donald James: *World's End: A Memoir of a Blitz Childhood*. Century, 2005.

2

The First Residents and their World
1931-1961

Cast List

Born for the most part in the final decades of the Victorian age, these early Swan Courters —apart from the three Americans — spent their formative years in the sunny uplands of Edwardian England. All but four lived to see the nineteen-sixties shred the last scraps of the world they were born into. Four passed the millennium. Most were at the peak of their creative lives during their Swan Court years.

The First Residents and their World

The Early Years: 1931-1940

Edward McKnight Kauffer	artist and graphic designer
Marion Dorn	textile and carpet designer
Peter Gregory	publisher, patron and art collector
Francis Bruguière	Modernist photographer
Rosalinde Fuller	actress, singer and artist's muse
Antony Gibbons Grinling	sculptor and businessman
The Hon. Bryan Guinness	novelist, poet and reluctant 'Bright Young Thing'
Francis Lorne	Modernist architect
Ernest Milton	classical actor
Naomi Royde Smith	literary editor, novelist and salon hostess
Nancy O'Neil	actress and movie star
The Earl of Jersey	art collector
Virginia Cherrill	'Chaplin's girl', Hollywood star and socialite
Sir Lewis Casson	actor and theatre director
Dame Sybil Thorndike	actress and social campaigner
John Hayward	anthologist and man of letters
Peter Eckersley	pioneer of radio and public service broadcasting
Dorothy Eckersley	political hostess and Nazi sympathiser
Arthur Bryant	popular historian and admirer of Hitler
The Hon. Thomas Freeman Mitford	'the Mitford boy'

The War Years and After: 1941–1961

Lesley Blanch	writer and Russophile
Anne Scott-James	journalist
Macdonald Hastings	journalist and broadcaster
Denis Thatcher	businessman
Margaret Thatcher	chemist, lawyer and aspiring politician
Dame Agatha Christie	crime writer
Sir Max Mallowan	archaeologist

The First Residents and their World

T**he idea for this book began one summer** evening in 2014 when I was invited to one of Swan Court's eighth-floor studios for a drink. It was warm and sunny, and we sat with our glasses of wine on the little walkway that runs around three sides of the flat. The roofs of South London stretched away into the distance, perhaps even to the Surrey hills. My hosts, both architects, handed me a book with a bright yellow cover. Slanted across the top was an angular black and white design of birds in flight, curiously familiar. The book fell open at a photograph of a youngish man standing behind a desk, eyes slanted away from the camera, deep in thought. This was my first proper meeting with the artist and designer Edward McKnight Kauffer, photographed in the studio I was now visiting.

Edward McKnight Kauffer at work in flat 141, during his last year in Swan Court. The Artist, 1939.

The photograph is dated March 1939, just over a year before Kauffer and his partner, the textile designer Marion Dorn, listed as aliens, made a dash for it across the Atlantic in the summer of 1940, back to their native America. Perhaps his thoughtful expression indicates the sense of an ending; his departure chopped off a life he loved and a dazzling London career in which he'd gone from washing dishes for a living in 1915 to near-legendary status in the thirties as one of the country's top graphic designers. He would never see England again, but his eight years living and working in Swan Court were stimulating and companionable, surrounded by a like-minded mix of friends and neighbours, and with links through work and social life to residents in other parts of the block.

Swan Court opened its doors to these first tenants in the autumn of 1931. In many ways it was an inauspicious time for a new venture. The country's economic plight was pressing and on September 21st a shocked nation was told that Britain had come off the Gold Standard. An historic date, said *The Economist* the following Saturday, marking the end of an epoch in the world's financial and economic development. In the days that followed, Continental resorts were emptied of their rich patrons as the well-heeled British ran for home. The Duke of Connaught, accustomed to wintering in Cap Ferrat, announced he was off to Sidmouth. The nation tightened its belt and talked of economies. The General Election of October 27th saw the Labour government wiped out and a Tory-dominated National Administration under Labour's Ramsay MacDonald emerging from the wreckage.

During 1932, as Swan Court's flats began to fill up, the streets of London bore depressing witness to the nation's economic problems. Fourteen years after the ending of the Great War, limbless veterans were still selling matches on street corners and between three and four million people were out of work. Throughout the decade a series of hunger marches from the provinces brought Londoners face to face with thousands of unemployed and disaffected workers. The sight of men without work, said Roy Hattersley, was the abiding tragedy of the inter-war years, and one which etched itself into the British collective memory.

The political upheavals fuelled a growing disillusion about the way the country was run. Governments seemed incapable of solving the problems. There had to be a better way of doing things, people said, as they sought comfort and inspiration in a raft of different ideas and philosophies. Swan Court had its admirers of Hitler's new Germany, many turning openly to right-wing politics nearer home. Bryan Guinness' wife Diana Mitford fell passionately in love with Oswald Mosley and his burgeoning British Union of Fascists. Her brother Tom, who lived in Swan Court from 1933, followed Diana and their sister Unity, all three visiting Germany regularly through the thirties and falling victim to the specious charms of the Nazi regime. Arthur Bryant used his newly won literary status to promote the cause, publishing paeans of praise for the new German Chancellor and recommending his *Mein Kampf* as required reading. Dorothy Eckersley tasted everything on the left of the political spectrum before veering off to the Fascists and disappearing to what was to become a notorious existence in war-time Berlin.

For John Hayward, who arrived in Swan Court in the late thirties, the decade following the First World War had been an aimless ragtime world, hectic, fearful and neurotic. It was a good description of an age of frenzied partying that has passed into legend, the scandalous antics of the 'Bright Young People' horrifying their parents and filling the gossip columns. Now, as the generation that had grown up with the century entered its third decade, the national mood was changing, the excesses of the party crowd condemned in the press as bad taste in an era scarred by hunger marches.

In the late twenties, Bryan and Diana Guinness had been a gilded couple at the very heart of the upper-class party set, but by the summer of 1932, when Diana gave a ball for her sister Unity in Cheyne Walk, the public mood was very different. Arriving at the house with Diana's sister Nancy, cartoonist Osbert Lancaster noted the small crowd of onlookers; there was little press interest and none of the usual gasps of wonder at the saucily-dressed nymphs disgorging from taxis and skipping up the steps. Later that year, the very public break-up of the Guinness marriage was a symptom of the changing times. Guinness, disillusioned with the party scene, wanted a quieter life. His wife thought otherwise and skipped the marital home for her Fascist lover, subsequently shifting her abandoned husband into bachelor existence in his Swan Court refuge.

Despite the decade's political and economic uncertainty, people's daily lives were being transformed by new technology. Increasing numbers could afford cars, air travel was on its way to becoming a means of passenger transport and sea travel was all the rage. Vacuum cleaners had arrived and refrigerators were changing the way people shopped and ate, Swan Court's sleek all-electric kitchens an invitation to a more labour-saving life. Television was developing slowly, but the nation's major passion was radio. The age of the cat's whisker had passed; cheap wireless sets were now on sale at a price most people could afford. The 'hams', who loved the whole craft of radio, had been submerged in a flood of 'listeners'; the BBC's 2.1 million licence-holders in 1922 had grown to over nine million by the outbreak of war. Peter Eckersley's new neighbours in Swan Court, gathering round their wireless sets every evening, were living alongside the key figure in the development of radio and the public service broadcasting they now relished. His fall from grace at the BBC two years before had been widely publicised, and his arrival in the block with a glamorous new wife hinted at the story behind the headlines.

Outside the home, going to 'the pictures' was fast becoming the nation's weekly outing, giving people from all backgrounds an affordable and exciting escape from reality. Throughout the decade new cinemas sprang up in virtually every town, suburb or major new housing development. Swan Court's local, the opulent Gaumont Palace, opened its doors in the King's Road in 1934. Built on the site of cinematographer William Frieze-Greene's studio, the Gaumont seated 2,500 people and showed all the big Hollywood musicals so passionately loved by Dorothy Eckersley and her son James. Swan Court had its share of film actors too, with Ernest Milton appearing to acclaim in 1934 as Robespierre in Alexander Korda's *The Scarlet Pimpernel* with Lesley Howard, Merle Oberon and Raymond Massey. Ingénue Nancy O'Neil was regularly to be seen lighting up the screens in many 'quota quickies'. But the big star was Virginia Cherrill, known from 1931 to audiences around the world for her appearance as the blind girl in Charlie Chaplin's silent film *City Lights*, which premiered in London the February before Swan Court opened. Cherrill was still trailing clouds of glory when she arrived in the block in 1934, her off-screen appeal for British film-goers – and for her new neighbours – further enhanced since her very public marriage and recent break-up from Cary Grant.

Two other passions of the nineteen-thirties, speed and luxury, were nowhere better indulged than in the decade's great ocean-going liners. The Orient Line's ultra-modern *Orion*, launched in 1935, was a landmark in design history. It was the brainchild of one of the Line's junior directors, Colin (later Sir Colin) Anderson, a young man with an eye for design and quality. He threw out all the old ideas of what a liner should look like, rejecting veneered panelling, brass work and chintzes in favour of white metal at sea. Of the several artist-designers Anderson commissioned, the two who had the most impact, he said, were Edward McKnight Kauffer and Marion Dorn. Kauffer designed a huge engraved glass mirror for the *Orion* and gave general advice on all design know-how and typography. He produced posters, invitations, brochures and baggage tags for the *Orion* and her sister ship *Orcades II*, and both ships featured Dorn's first sea-going rugs and carpets. She was also commissioned by Cunard to design carpets for their new superliner, the *Queen Mary*, which launched in 1934.

Colin Anderson was one of the new breed of patron-businessmen which included London Underground's Frank Pick and Shell's Jack Beddington. Artistically sophisticated and with funds at their disposal, they set about drawing the decade's most interesting artists and designers into a mutually-rewarding relationship between commerce and the arts, developing a design language still alive today. Kauffer and Dorn, adept at nurturing work and social relationships with their patrons, produced some of the best designs of their careers. Their Swan Court friend and neighbour Francis Bruguière got in on the act, adding his distinctive avant-garde photography to advertisements for petrol and corsets. Another enthusiastic patron was Peter Gregory, chairman of art publisher Lund Humphries and later to be a Swan Court neighbour. Gregory made Kauffer the first design director of Lund Humphries, where he shared a studio with the Modernist photographer Man Ray. The company's exhibition gallery opened in December 1933 with a show dedicated to Kauffer and Francis Bruguière in surroundings partly designed by Marion Dorn.

To the inter-war generation, bent on throwing away the past and reinventing the world, it was exhilarating to embrace new technology and move with the times, but for the British, when it came to Modernism, caution was the order of the day. Writing in the *Architectural Review*, the Vorticist artist Percy Wyndham Lewis – a regular visitor to Swan Court – wrote that one swallower of the new forms of expression did not make a summer for the artist. For every swallower, he said, there were a thousand who violently rejected the 'bitter pill' of the most modern schools. To the more conservative in all walks of life, any kind of modernity in art, architecture, literature, dress or sexual mores was shocking, incomprehensible or even dangerous. As an admirer of Le Corbusier, Swan Court's Francis Lorne, like other architects, produced the occasional Modernist-inspired building while – with lucrative commissions in mind – working most of the time in more traditional styles. Sculptor Antony Gibbons Grinling, company director of distillers W&A Gilbey, had a fight on his hands when he suggested a Modernist architect for the firm's new headquarters. A good deal depended on presentation; McKnight Kauffer delighted the public with art they would have scorned in a gallery.

Behind closed doors, some Swan Court residents pursued the new and daring, whether in life or interior décor. Actress Rosalinde Fuller, energetic exponent of free love, regularly stripped off to pose alone and in company for her live-in lover Francis Bruguière. We have no description of their flat, but other interiors are on the record. Kauffer's studio, floored in white linoleum, was set off by Marion Dorn's Modernist rugs and curtains; Francis Lorne's flat sported the latest built-in furniture; the Eckersleys' was all glass and chromium; while architect Serge Chermayeff's design for Antony Gibbons Grinling's studio featured fashionable reflective surfaces to display his sculptures.

Movers and shakers of the arts world drift through the pages of biographies and memoirs as visitors to Swan Court.

Nancy Mitford visited her brother Tom and her ex-brother-in-law Bryan Guinness, of whom she was very fond. Evelyn Waugh was an old Oxford friend of Guinness and remained close to him after his marriage break-up. Filmmaker Oswall Blakeston was a regular visitor to Rosalinde Fuller and Francis Bruguière, as was Lance Sieveking, the BBC's assistant director of education and later their drama script editor. Art historian Kenneth (later Lord) Clark visited Ted Kauffer and Marion Dorn, marvelling at the exotic gadgetry Kauffer so loved. Another great friend, the poet and novelist Osbert Sitwell, often popped across from Carlyle Square. Percy Wyndham-Lewis, close friend and great admirer of Kauffer, was a frequent visitor to him and to the Eckersleys. Sculptor Henry Moore, the critic Herbert Read and many young up-and-coming artists visited Peter Gregory. Theatrical greats trooped up to flat 98 to see Dame Sybil Thorndike and her husband Lewis Casson. When it came to political figures, Oswald Mosley, popping down the King's Road from the new British Union of Fascists (BUF) headquarters, would have been hard to miss, but the young man with a razor-slash scar cleaving his face from lip to earlobe meant nothing in the nineteen-thirties. Yet after the war, when the nation's most notorious trial hit the headlines, Swan Court residents could dine out on stories of the day they'd seen William Joyce on his way to visit the scandalous Mrs Eckersley, by then herself in trouble with the authorities.

Amongst all the comings and goings, two defining voices of the age – T.S. Eliot and Aldous Huxley – stand out. John Hayward's story gives an insight into the impact of Eliot's Modernist writing from the publication of *The Lovesong of J Alfred Prufrock* in 1915. By the nineteen-thirties, Eliot's international reputation as poet, critic, and man of letters was growing apace and he'd won just about every honour the academic or literary world had to offer. His distinctive suited and hatted figure was frequently to be seen crossing the courtyard, when, as close friend to Ted Kauffer, Marion Dorn, Peter Gregory and John Hayward, he was on his way up to the South Block's top floors. He and Kauffer were very close for over twenty years, Eliot attempting unsuccessfully as war approached to persuade Kauffer to take out British citizenship. Their chat often centred on work, Kauffer being an artist Eliot trusted with designs for his book jackets. Naomi Royde-Smith, who had a taste for Modernist writing, was another resident who knew Eliot well. In earlier times, as literary editor of the influential *Westminster Gazette*, Naomi had championed the young and unknown poet and published his early works.

Aldous Huxley, friend and regular visitor to a number of Swan Court residents, was one of the leading intellectuals of the day and a lifelong seeker of truth, a quest he pursued vigorously by both intellectual and chemical means. When he began visiting his first cousin Peter Eckersley in 1932, Huxley was riding high following the publication of his dystopian novel *Brave New World*. He was a friend and admirer of Ted Kauffer, writing a percipient introduction to the catalogue for the 1937 exhibition of Kauffer's posters in the Museum of Modern Art in New York. He and Kauffer became close and corresponded regularly after Kauffer and Dorn had returned to the United States in 1940. Huxley had also been a friend of Naomi Royde-Smith since the early twenties, when he'd been one of a number of lodgers in her South Kensington home. There's a possible literary connection too between Huxley and Virginia Cherrill. Three years after he moved to California in 1936, Huxley published his novel *After Many a Summer Dies the Swan*, an exposé of what he saw as the superficiality of American culture and its obsession with youth. The main character, Joe Stoyte, is a sixty-year-old millionaire who builds himself an opulent castle stuffed with works of art where, in his efforts to live forever, he enjoys the favours of a young starlet called Virginia. The characters were popularly supposed at the time to be modelled on the newspaper tycoon Randolph Hearst and his girlfriend, film star Marion Davies. Cherrill's biographer Miranda Seymour suggests that Huxley's originals could well be Virginia Cherrill and Joe Adler, the rich semi-paralysed uncle-by-marriage who invited her to Hollywood and took her under his wing. Huxley would have been familiar with the legendary story of Cherrill's arrival in Hollywood and the exotic social life she enjoyed in the company of her adoring 'Uncle Joe'. Maybe Cherill was less wholesome and innocent than she suggested when reviewing her life decades later.

In the thirties, the continuing connectedness of Chelsea's cultural life was still to be seen in the artistic and literary salons, which continued to flourish in and around the King's Road until the start of the Second World War. From Swan Court, a short stroll took you to the drawing rooms of two of London's best-known hostesses, regularly visited by a number of Swan Court residents. From 1922, Lady Sybil Colefax had presided over one of the most celebrated salons of the age at Argyll House, 211 King's Road, where she entertained a stream of fashionable figures ranging from Winston Churchill to Cole Porter. John Hayward thought Lady Sybil the best and possibly the cleverest hostess in London at the time, although he found the occasions rather too full of noise and hubbub. Next door at 213, interior decorator Syrie Maugham, estranged wife of novelist Somerset Maugham, turned a narrow Georgian terraced house into the last word in nineteen-thirties' chic. Colefax and Maugham kept up a friendly rivalry, both in the interior decorating business and in the social status of their hordes of fashionable visitors. Maugham, who enjoyed the company of younger people, collected around her a coterie of new talent that included Marion Dorn, Noel Coward, Oliver Messel, Cecil Beaton and Beverley Nichols.

A little further down the King's Road were other popular gathering-places. At 2 Carlyle Square, Kauffer's close friend Osbert Sitwell and his sister Edith exercised a powerfully eccentric influence over cultural life, their acquaintances ranging from Oscar Wilde's old friend Robbie Ross to Jean Cocteau and Pablo Picasso. Especially fancied by artists was 15 The Vale, home of American painter Ethel Sands and her lifelong partner, the artist Nan Hudson. Walter Sickert, Augustus John and Henry James had been regular attendees at her salon, which remained an important meeting-place until the war. It all came to an end in the Blitz, when the house, which contained mosaics and murals she had commissioned from Boris Anrep, was destroyed by a parachute mine. Another favourite gathering-place was the men-only Chelsea Arts Club at 143 Old Church Street, where Kauffer had been a member since 1916.

Before John Hayward moved to Swan Court, Thursday evenings in his Kensington home were a haven for writers and bibliophiles, home-grown and international. Paul Valéry, the most renowned of contemporary French poets, described Hayward's gatherings as a centre of civilisation where, in an era of barbarians, you could see human faces. Naomi Royde-Smith, a well-known hostess in the nineteen-twenties, was 'at home' every week in Princes Gardens to a range of well-regarded literary figures, where Naomi's bewitched lover, the poet Walter de la Mare, was among many who succumbed to the charms of their blowsily beautiful hostess. By the time she reached her eighth-floor perch in Swan Court she had swapped her role as party-giver for the comforts of the married state and a new life as a novelist, leaving Dorothy Eckersley to keep the flame alive with her soirées in flat 82, popular with those who fancied their cocktails served with more than a dash of politics.

The War Years and After: 1941-1961

In 1939, with the onset of the 'Phoney War' and the threat of bombing, Swan Court's early residents began to move away from central London. Bryan Guinness and his new wife, Francis Bruguière and Rosalinde Fuller, the Miltons and Nancy O'Neil headed for the country. John Hayward found sanctuary in Cambridge and Virginia Cherrill came to rest in Richmond. Tom Mitford, Anthony Gibbons Grinling and the Earl of Jersey joined the army. McKnight Kauffer and Marion Dorn returned to America, while Dorothy Eckersley and her son James decamped to what was to prove a risky life in Berlin.

Three residents stayed put. Peter Gregory moved next door into Kauffer's old studio, working throughout the war in the Ministry of Information and remaining in the flat until his death in 1959. Dame Sybil Thorndike and Lewis Casson, who had moved into flat 98 in 1938, left briefly after a bomb fell behind the North Block on September 9th 1940, returning when the services were restored. Swan Court suffered no loss of life, but the same afternoon saw fifty-six people killed by direct hits in Beaufort and Bramerton Streets. By the end of the war, eight hundred and eighteen people had been killed in Chelsea, with dozens injured and hundreds of buildings damaged or destroyed.

From 1940, flat 69 became a convenient perch for three writers, with the colourfully eccentric Lesley Blanch followed by journalists Anne Scott-James and Macdonald Hastings. Peace brought Dame Agatha Christie to flat 48, while, four floors above, businessman Denis Thatcher lived alone in flat 112 until broken of his bachelor habits by the domestic tyranny of his new bride.

In the early post-war years, shabby Bohemian Chelsea was still a haven for cash-strapped artists and students. Laurie

Lee remembered the workmen's cafés serving kipper teas for a shilling and the scruffy pubs where dukes, lords, actors, writers, builders' labourers, policemen and crooks mingled with artists, both the struggling and the famous. But there were, said Lee, some remnants of the elegance of pre-war Chelsea; Osbert and Edith Sitwell wandering about in Carlyle Square, Sir Alfred Munnings in hacking jacket and jodhpurs striking the railings with his riding crop, and T.S. Eliot still to be seen pushing John Hayward round the streets in his wheelchair. A tiny flourish perhaps, but the days of the salonnières were over, that particular kind of social connectedness gone. And by the nineteen-sixties, as the King's Road began to fill up with Mods and Rockers, Teds, Skinheads, and flocks of mini-skirted girls, the Chelsea in which Swan Court had opened its doors had passed the point of no return.

MAIN SOURCES

Décharné, Max: *King's Road: The Rise and Fall of the Hippest Street in the World*. Weidenfeld & Nicolson, 2005.

Gardiner, Juliet: *The Thirties: An Intimate History*. HarperPress, 2010.

Hattersley, Roy: *Borrowed Time: The Story of Britain Between the Wars*. Little Brown, 2007.

Huxley, Aldous: *After Many a Summer Dies the Swan*. Chatto and Windus, 1939.

Lee, Laurie: 'Laurie Lee's Chelsea' in *The Illustrated London News*, December, 1987.

Pugh, Martin: *We Danced all Night: A Social History of Britain Between the Wars*. Bodley Head, 2008.

Victoria County History, Vol XII 2005.

3

The Blue Plaque Couple
Edward McKnight Kauffer (1890-1954)
Marion Dorn (1896-1964)
Flat 139/141, 1931-1940

The Blue Plaque Couple

In August 1914, twenty-four-year-old American Edward McKnight Kauffer – Ted to his friends – and his young pianist wife Grace arrived in England. First in Newcastle and then in London, he tramped the streets trying to sell designs and ideas for posters, his evenings spent dishwashing to keep them afloat. Just five years later, the posters he was producing for the London Underground would make him a household name.

Flip through any book of his designs and you can see why. With dazzling line and colour, powerful symbolism and an unparalleled combination of artistic brilliance and quirky intellect, nothing with Kauffer is ever ordinary. As his friend and admirer Aldous Huxley pointed out, Kauffer's genius was to make his designs symbolic of the thing being advertised, unlike most advertising artists who used designs symbolic of sex and money to promote absolutely anything from refrigerators to holiday resorts. Imagine the effect on travellers when his clever joyous images sang out at them from hoardings and station platforms, lighting up the urban landscape of London in the drab years during and after the First World War. The travelling public – for the most part unaware that it was being introduced to modern art – became so attached to Kauffer's work that one advertiser, the dyers and cleaners Eastman & Sons, produced a sticker to be used on temporarily empty sites. It read 'A new McKnight Kauffer poster will be here shortly'. Kauffer proudly kept one of these for the rest of his life.

The red-headed American boy from a poor background in Evansville, Indiana, had drawn since he was old enough to hold a pencil. Raised by a single mother, he left school early and picked a living doing odd jobs, plus scene-painting in the Evansville opera house. By 1910 he was working in a San Francisco bookstore and studying art in the evenings. Here

McKnight Kauffer, photographed by his Swan Court neighbour Francis Bruguière, circa 1933.

he met his first patron, Professor Joseph E McKnight, who paid for him to study art in Paris. Adding McKnight's name to his own in thanks to his patron, the twenty-year-old set off for Europe and a crash course in what was happening in the modern art world.

Passing through Chicago, he caught the Armory Show, an exhibition that had caused a huge sensation when it opened in New York. The American art establishment, now just about comfortable with the French Impressionists, was brought up short and sharp by Cézanne, Matisse and other Fauves, by Cubism with Braque and Picasso and by Kandinsky and the German Expressionists. The works caused public outrage, but for the young Kauffer they were a revelation. By 1913 he was in Paris, where Modernism was bursting out from the shadows into popular culture. Kauffer absorbed everything from Van Gogh to the works of the Italian Futurists, reaching England in 1915 in a ferment of ideas and images.

T.S. Eliot, later to be a great friend, attributed much of Kauffer's startling career to his ability to find and keep enlightened patrons. London provided him with four people in particular – one a Swan Court neighbour – who became key players in his life, their encouragement and support ensuring his pre-eminence in inter-war developments in the visual language of advertising. Far more than just useful business acquaintances with work in their gift, they became the lynchpins of a circle of creative friends and neighbours who did much to sustain Kauffer's muse and his social life during his twenty-five years in London.

His first patron and mentor was Frank Pick, then Assistant Joint Manager of the London Underground, a man of enlightened artistic sensibility who took a chance on the impoverished young artist and commissioned a series of posters advertising attractive open spaces on the fringes of London that could be visited by underground or bus. Kauffer's first posters, *In Watford* and *Oxhey Woods*, appeared in 1915, with *Reigate: Route 160* and *North Downs* a year later. Pick subsequently commissioned some of the most eminent artists working in the inter-war years, including Man Ray, Graham Sutherland, Hans

Schleger, Tom Eckersley and László Moholy-Nagy. Much of Pick's chosen design has become embedded in English culture, such as the 1910 red, white and blue roundel that symbolises the London Underground and the diagrammatic map used from 1933. Pick immediately recognised Kauffer's brilliance in manipulating the tricky relationship between art and commerce, and having bagged such a major patron and client, Kauffer had come home; he would never be without a commission again during his years in England.

Another early supporter was publisher, typographer and poet Francis (later Sir Francis) Meynell, who talent-spotted Kauffer through what has become the most famous single image of his oeuvre. *Flight*, originally a woodcut, went through various versions in print from 1917, but only took off when Meynell used it to headline his spectacular advertising campaign that launched the Labour newspaper the *Daily Herald*. On the last day of March 1919 the ads hit the street,

| *Flight, woodcut, 1917.*

the flight of angular black and white birds vivid against the butter-yellow background, topping the caption 'Soaring to Success! – the Early Bird'. It was an immediate hit.

The legendary Jack Beddington, director of the newly-formed Shell-Mex BP, became a major patron and friend from the late nineteen-twenties. A warm and clubbable man, Beddington was a perspicacious collector of modern art, seeing all the new shows, buying from promising unknowns and covering his walls with works by Wyndham Lewis, Sickert, David Bomberg and LS Lowry, among many others. Beddington used his passion for art and design, photography, film and literature in his work for Shell, sponsoring avant-garde films and commissioning talented newcomers like the illustrator Nicholas Bentley, the artist Paul Nash and the young poet and writer John Betjeman, who began the renowned series of Shell County Guides. Now Kauffer joined this stable of artists, turning out a stream of exceptional posters for Shell products over the next years. Beddington became a close personal friend, the two frequently dining together at the Café Royal and corresponding privately for the rest of Kauffer's life.

Peter Gregory, chairman of art publishers Lund Humphries and later to be an immediate neighbour in Swan Court, met Kauffer around 1920, commissioning a design from him for one of the firm's series of artists' Christmas cards. Gregory, an indefatigable promoter, supporter and befriender of many gifted artists, mounted a major exhibition of Kauffer's work in Lund Humphries' gallery in 1935. The show became a fashionable rendezvous for art-minded London and was widely reviewed. *The Scotsman* called Kauffer 'the Picasso of advertising design', while *The Guardian* compared him to Noël Coward in the way his exciting personality had entered into the life of the times. Following the show, the young Anthony

Blunt – later Surveyor of the Queen's Pictures and head of the Courtauld Institute of Art – said it was nonsense to look on Kauffer as a minor artist simply because he did many varied things and was not purely a painter or sculptor. 'If he is minor, then who is major?' asked Blunt. As Francis Meynell wrote later, Kauffer was an example of the abandoned truth that art is indivisible: 'a man with the root of the matter in him can paint or design rugs or make posters or illustrate books or decorate a room or parti-colour a car or scheme an advertisement'. Sadly, the parti-coloured car, which Kauffer did for Meynell, did not survive.

Perhaps with happy memories of painting sets in the Evansville Opera House, Kauffer made occasional forays into stage design. In 1919, the dancer Margaret Morris had set up the Arts League of Service from her Chelsea studio – now home to the American home and fashion store Anthropologie – just across Flood Street from where, a decade later, Swan Court would rise from the ashes of Wolsey's old workshops. The League aimed to channel energies into the arts after four years of war, and its first project was a lecture series, with T.S. Eliot on poetry, Wyndham Lewis on painting, Eugene Goosens on music and Morris herself on dancing. Kauffer immediately joined the Artists sub-committee, contributing an article on poster design to the League and regularly designing their sets, costumes and posters.

In his Swan Court years, Kauffer also designed sets and costumes for his soon-to-be neighbour Ernest Milton's *Othello* in 1932, followed by Gordon Daviot's *Queen of Scots* for John Gielgud in 1934. Then, three years later, came his sets and red, black and white costumes for Ninette de Valois' legendary production of *Checkmate* for the Vic-Wells Ballet. First performed at the Theatre de Champs Elysée in Paris with Constant Lambert conducting, the premier dancers included Robert Helpmann, Frederick Ashton and Michael Somes, plus an eighteen-year-old Margot Fonteyn as one of the Pawns in the corps de ballet. In an explosion of colour, Kauffer's bold modern designs perfectly matched de Valois' sharp choreography and Sir Arthur Bliss' dramatic score. Sadly, the original costumes had to be abandoned in Holland in May 1940 as the Vic-Wells fled the German invasion. After the war, Kauffer re-created them all, the Pawns missing their elegant black gloves in the face of post-war shortages. In a link down the years to the Swan Court of today, current resident Kathryn Wade, then a Royal Ballet soloist, was second cast to Natalia Makarova as the Black Queen in 1975. The de Valois production of *Checkmate*, now over eighty years old, remains a staple of the Birmingham Royal Ballet's repertoire. The costumes look as good as ever, and this classic of nineteen-thirties' style is relished by twenty-first-century audiences.

Kauffer's marriage had foundered in 1923 when he left Grace and their small daughter to set up home with Marion Dorn. Eight years later, he and Dorn became the first occupants of the double studio on the south-western corner of Swan Court. They made a glamorous couple. Kauffer's patron, the Orient Line's chairman Colin Anderson, found him a pleasure to the eye, like a slim russet eagle, his clothes elegant and dégagé. He and the handsome dark-haired Dorn were 'Henry Jamesian' Americans, said Diana Mosley, who remembered them, very tall and distinguished, attending the parties she gave in Buckingham Street when she was married to Bryan Guinness.

Intense and obsessive, Kauffer was tidy to the point of mania, perhaps a disappointment to anyone who felt that artists should display a Bohemian disregard for domestic niceties. There was nothing careless in how he lived or the arrangement of the Swan Court studio. The built-in furniture was dusted twice each day and the tools of Kauffer's trade were immaculately arranged, pens and pencils in impeccable order, shelves filled with box files neatly named for each client. His assistant, Sidney Garrad, said Kauffer knew at once if so much as a pencil had been moved and would immediately return it to its rightful place. This orderliness extended to his clothes. He did not find it funny when, for a joke, neighbour Francis Bruguière and his friend the film-maker Oswald Blakeston muddled up the sequence of silk handkerchiefs that he'd laid out ready for each day of the coming week. Whether Dorn found this compulsive tidiness somewhat trying is not known.

| *A corner of McKnight Kauffer's studio, with Marion Dorn's curtains at the window.*

Did she enjoy living with all the gadgets he so loved, or having to give house-room to his collection of more than a thousand gramophone records? Although generally described as a gentle, loveable character, the obsessive aspects of his personality may have been difficult for a co-habitee. The writer and aesthete Harold Acton described how people could sap Kauffer's energy, making him morose and misanthropic and giving the attractive, sociable Dorn the irksome duty of keeping them away. Such moments may well have ruffled domestic harmony. Whatever the reasons, theirs was a volatile relationship and every so often the two of them separated temporarily with the aim of 'finding each other' again.

Known for her good looks and sense of humour, Marion Dorn was in every way Kauffer's equal as a designer. Much has been written about her work, but no biography has yet emerged and we know a good deal less of her personal life and character than we do of Kauffer's. Born and brought up in California, she studied graphic arts at Stanford University and in 1919, at the age of twenty-three, married one of her professors, the artist Henry Varnum Poor, with whom she shared a studio in San Francisco and then New York. After four years of marriage she divorced Poor and moved to London, where she settled down to work, building a top-flight reputation for designing wallpaper, graphics and interiors as well as her trademark rugs and textile designs. Her carpets found their way to world-famous hotels such as the Berkeley, the Savoy and Claridges in London, and to the Art Deco masterpiece, the Midland Hotel in Morecambe. Her rugs, for which she was best known, were conceived and marketed as limited-edition fine art productions. She was commissioned by Cunard to design carpets for the *Queen Mary*, by the Orient Line for *Orion* and *Orcades II*, and by London Transport for moquette for train seating.

| *Marion Dorn, photographed by Edward McKnight Kauffer, 1930s.*

She worked with top decorators of the day, designing a huge patterned rug for Syrie Maugham's famous all-white Chelsea drawing-room, which sparked a passion for white furnishings around the country. It's said the irascible Maugham threw an appropriately white satin bedroom slipper at Dorn in a fit of temper one day, but the rug survived to become an integral part of an interior that has passed into design history. She also worked for two Swan Court neighbours, designing costumes for actor Ernest Milton and a rug for sculptor Antony Gibbons Grinling's studio.

Dorn, also an excellent business woman, set up her company, Marion Dorn Ltd, in 1934. It became a great commercial success, the showroom and studio just off Bond Street a fashionable and stimulating place to visit in thirties' London. Despite this, her reputation was somewhat overshadowed by Kauffer's – at the time and since – largely because she chose to work almost exclusively in textiles and interior design, areas traditionally regarded as 'decorative' and 'female' rather than in any way as pure art.

Those in the know thought otherwise about Dorn's work. They put her in the same bracket as the decade's leading Modernist architects and she was sought after as collaborator by top practitioners of the day, such as Oliver Hill, Robert Lutyens, Serge Chermayeff, Eric Mendelsohn, Wells Coates, and Brian O'Rorke, who recognised her abstract patterned rugs as far more than warm coverings for bare floors or accompaniments to colour schemes. Even in photographs you can see the weight and focus her carpets give to the rooms they were designed for; take them away and the scheme falls apart. Her work changed the perceived importance of textiles in interior design, making them key elements rather than decorative add-ons.

A shrewd self-publicist, Dorn attracted a fashionable clientele – Noël Coward was a great fan – and collaborators such as Graham Sutherland, who exhibited ceramics in her showroom in 1939. However, there's no doubt that hitching her wagon to her live-in lover's ascendant star did her no harm. Moving into Kauffer's inter-connected world brought her some excellent introductions, to say nothing of an engaging social life. Her client list echoed his to a significant extent and they often worked on joint projects.

In 1938, Kauffer and Dorn rented a small Regency cottage tucked into a fold of the Chiltern Hills and set about re-decorating it and making a garden. A quick journey by car from Swan Court and near to Jack Beddington's country house, it was their dream retreat, but sadly not to last. When war was declared in 1939, as aliens they faced a raft of bureaucratic difficulties, not least the need to obtain a permit every time they wished to travel to Buckinghamshire. Work began to dry up. Kauffer, keen to help the war effort, was appalled to find himself doing pointless tasks for the Ministry of Information. They were becoming liabilities, consuming more than they could contribute, and soon there might be no more ships crossing the Atlantic. On July 1st 1940, Kauffer's friend, the graphic designer Hans Schleger, dialled Flaxman 0217 and spoke to the maid. They've gone, she told him. And so they had, leaving the studio and everything in it at a moment's notice, running for the docks with twenty-five pounds each and a few personal belongings – though Dorn somehow managed to take her harpsichord. They reached Ireland in time to catch the *SS Washington* bound for New York.

Life in Manhattan with no money was far from a joke. Dorn made batik scarves and sold them on the streets to pay the bills. Kauffer went through the first winter with a raincoat and one pair of shoes, some book jacket design work bringing in a tiny income. Mourning the loss of his work and social life in London, his letters to friends in England expressed his sense of deprivation and exile, and the following summer he had a breakdown. Over the next years his career revived to a certain extent, largely through the support of one last patron and client, Bernard Waldman, which resulted in a superb set of over thirty posters for American Airlines in the post-war years. In truth he never really settled in America, finding the commercialism of the New York advertising world less than congenial and, as he put it himself, feeling forever betwixt and between, an eternal expatriate mired in mid-Atlantic.

Dorn's career blossomed and her status as the main earner in the partnership proved a source of dissension in their relationship. They married in 1950 but lived very separate lives. His last years were deeply unhappy, immersed in heavy drinking and cut off from old friends who felt powerless to help. He died in 1954. Dorn spent her last years in Tangier and died in 1964.

MAIN SOURCES

Conversations with Simon Rendall, McKnight Kauffer's grandson.

Acton, Harold: *Memoirs of an Aesthete*. Methuen, 1948.

Blunt, Anthony: *The Spectator*, April 1935.

Boydell, Christine: *The Architect of Floors: Modernism, Art and Marion Dorn Designs*. RIBA Heinz Gallery, November 1996.

Boydell, Christine: 'The Decorative Imperative: Marion Dorn's Textiles and Modernism' in *The Journal of the Decorative Arts Society 1850–the Present*, No.19 1995.

Guise, Barry and Brook, Pam: *The Midland Hotel: Morecombe's White Hope*. Palatine Books, 2007.

Haworth-Booth, Mark: *E. McKnight Kauffer: A Designer and his Public*. V&A Publications, 2005. See also Haworth-Booth's Kauffer essay in *The Oxford Dictionary of National Biography*.

Huxley, Aldous: 1937 Museum of Modern Art exhibition catalogue.

Klaidman, Stephen: *Sydney and Violet: Their Life with T.S. Eliot, Proust, Joyce and the Excruciatingly Irascible Wyndham Lewis*. Doubleday, 2013.

Meynell, Francis: *My Lives*. Bodley Head, 1971.

Pevsner, Nikolaus: 'Frank Pick'. In *Studies in Art, Architecture and Design, Vol 2: Victorian and After*. Thames & Hudson, 1968.

Saler, Michael: *The Avant-Garde in Inter-War England: Medieval Modernism and the London Underground*. Oxford University Press, 2001.

Todd, D: 'Marion Dorn: Architect of Floors' in *The Architectural Review* 72, 1932.

Webb, Brian, and Skipwith, Peyton: *Design: E. McKnight Kauffer*. Antique Collectors' Club, 2007.

4

The Artists' Friend
*Eric Craven (Peter) Gregory
(1888-1959)
Flats 133 and 139/141
1934-1959*

IN THE SPRING OF 2019, SIX YOUNG POETS BECAME THE latest in a glittering list to pull off one of poetry's most highly regarded prizes. The Gregory Poetry Awards, funded by a legacy from Peter Gregory and given annually since 1960, are open to poets under thirty years old who submit collections of up to thirty poems to a panel of distinguished judges. The prize money in today's world is not large – £24,000 per year divided between a number of contestants – but the prestige is considerable. Previous winners include Seamus Heaney, Kathleen Jamie and Alice Oswald, to say nothing of three Poets Laureate – Andrew

Peter Gregory (right), photographed by Lee Miller, with her husband, artist and writer Sir Roland Penrose (left) and sculptor Henry Moore (centre) in St. Mark's Square for the 1948 Venice Bienniale.

Motion, Carol Ann Duffy and the present incumbent, Simon Armitage. The list reads like a *Who's Who* of British poetry and the judges each year are among the most admired of their generation. In 1960, the poet Christopher Levenson, first winner of the Award, submitted his work to a panel that included T.S. Eliot. Levenson recalled afterwards that as well as his award, Eliot gave him some advice — not the literary wisdom he might have expected, but guidance on how to avoid paying tax on his prize money. Peter Gregory, ever appreciative of the financial struggles of young writers and artists, might well have approved.

Gregory's heart was in the arts, but he spent a working lifetime in business, joining the Bradford firm of printers and publishers Lund Humphries in 1911. After the war he became chairman, a position he held until his death in 1959. It was a career perfectly suited to a man with his artistic sensibilities. Lund Humphries had a name for fine typography and was very well aware of its potential for commercial design. Peter Gregory's astute eye, irrepressible energy and confirmed belief in English Modernism was a compelling combination, and from the end of the thirties he geared the list increasingly to the production of high-end books on modern British artists. In the forties and fifties came the first illustrated monographs on leading British artists, among them Henry Moore, Ben Nicholson and Paul Nash. Magnificent volumes, said the critic Herbert Read. Towards the end of Gregory's life, Lund Humphries was publishing the best of international Modernism while at the same time pushing modern British artists firmly into the mainstream of international contemporary art. Gregory's time at Lund Humphries is well-documented on their website in Valerie Holman's history of the company.

After the war, Gregory launched into a series of imaginative projects aimed at helping artists and spreading the idea of modern art as part of everyday life. First up were the Fellowships in the Creative Arts at Leeds University. While the scheme aimed to give young artists time and space to develop their work, Gregory's real objectives were to bring the artists into touch with the youth of the country and with the needs of the community. His dream was that the Fellowships would go some way towards closing what he saw as a great gap between art and society.

The initial Fellowships were in painting, sculpture, poetry and music. To oversee the scheme, Gregory set up an Advisory Committee composed of a small group of friends. Meetings, mostly over dinner, were held in Swan Court, where T.S. Eliot, Henry Moore, Herbert Read and the Leeds Professor of English Literature, Bonamy Dobrée, would gather round the table arguing for and against candidates for Fellowships. There was a common resolve never to relax standards. No sanctuary for the second-rate, insisted Herbert Read. 'I don't think you are going to enhance the prestige of the University by having some obscure minor poet hanging round the place – or a Bloomsbury beard or a Welsh inebriate or a Scottish potwalloper.'

Peter Gregory supported the Fellowships by covenanting £1,700 out of his income annually for the first nine years, with the university picking up the tab thereafter. Although the scheme ran into funding problems in the eighties and was eventually discontinued, the seeds had been sown with great benefit to the creative life of both town and gown. In Leeds, the presence of the Fellows had produced an ongoing buzz of interest and excitement about modern art. The whole idea of the Fellowships immediately attracted interest elsewhere at home and abroad, and in due course other universities followed suit. 'Writers in residence' are now commonplace: Gregory's Poetry Fellowship in 1946 was the first such scheme in any British university.

In 1946, Gregory got together with a small group of artists and patrons – including the artist, historian and poet Roland Penrose, philanthropist and collector Peter Watson, and Herbert Read – to found the Institute of Contemporary Arts (ICA) as a showcase for the work of living artists in a wide variety of contemporary art forms. Gregory became Honorary Treasurer, and when the ICA's first landmark exhibition, Forty Years of Modern Art, was proposed in 1947, he agreed to print the catalogue and guarantee the Institute against financial loss. By the fifties, the ICA electrified the art scene with a series of ground-breaking exhibitions, including those by Francis Bacon, Lucien Freud and Pablo Picasso. In 1968 it moved to premises in the Mall, where it flourishes to this day.

Gregory was also a member of the Arts Panel of the Arts Council, Honorary Secretary of the Contemporary Art Society from 1955 to 1958, a Director of *The Burlington Magazine*, and Governor of Chelsea Polytechnic, St. Martin's School of Art and Bath Academy of Art.

This extraordinary and lovable man was a powerhouse of creative ideas that have had a life far beyond his own, yet the epithet 'self-effacing' crops up over and over again in everything written and quoted about Peter Gregory. He never blew his own trumpet and it was only after his death in 1959 that even close friends realised the extent of his benefactions. His going, wrote his great friend the architect Jane Drew, was an irreplaceable loss to the sculptors, artists and poets of this country. He befriended them, bought their work and gave them thoughtful encouragement at a time when they most needed it. At a very early stage in their careers he supported, among countless others, Ben Nicolson, Barbara Hepworth, Lyn Chadwick, Victor Pasmore and Eduardo Paolozzi. The sculptor Henry Moore, unknown when they first met, acknowledged the enormous debt he and generations of younger sculptors owed to Gregory for his championship.

Gregory delighted in the personal friendships that flowed from his perspicacious talent-spotting. First in flat 133 and then for the rest of his life in Kauffer and Dorn's old studio, 141, his jumbled book-filled Swan Court homes overflowed with the work of gifted young artists, spotted long before they came to public recognition. Unlike many collectors, who tend as they get older to continue patronising the artists of their own generation, Peter Gregory constantly embraced new ideas. A week before his death he was doing the rounds of studios and galleries, showing enthusiasm and understanding for painters and sculptors maybe half a century younger than himself, and never ceasing to help anyone whose work he admired, just as he had done for McKnight Kauffer and Francis Bruguière two decades earlier when they were neighbours.

Gregory never married, but he went through life collecting devoted friends across the generations. His memorial service in St. Luke's, Sydney Street, overflowed the church. He was, as Jane Drew said, a most unusual man, kind, merry and self-effacing, with a quality of being lovable as well as respected. In Swan Court he must have been the best of neighbours.

Perhaps the last word should go to Gregory's close friend and committed supporter, CR Morris, Vice-Chancellor of Leeds University from 1948 to 1963:

'He took his own pleasure largely from the friendship of creative artists – poets, painters, sculptors, architects… He had great faith in youth, as well as in knowledge and in beauty and he was confident that something could be done… in the last year or two of his life he really felt that something had been done – and from this thought he took great pleasure.'

MAIN SOURCES

Diaper, Valerie: article in *The British Vision of World Art* by Herbert Read, Leeds City Art Galleries in association with the Henry Moore Foundation. Lund Humphries, 1993.

See references to Peter Gregory in Haworth-Booth, Mark: *E. McKnight Kauffer: A Designer and his Public*. V&A Publications, 2005.

Holman, Valerie: *A Short History of Lund Humphries*. Lund Humphries, January 2014.

5

The Photographer and his Muse

Francis Joseph Bruguière (1879-1945)
Rosalinde Fuller OBE (1892-1982)
Flat 101 1932-1940

IN THE AUTUMN OF 1919, A NEAR-UNKNOWN WRITER called F. Scott Fitzgerald was in New York for the publication of his first novel, *This Side of Paradise*. One evening at a crowded party in the Plaza Hotel, he spotted a striking dark-haired girl with huge eyes and a bold, adventurous look. She was English, an actress and singer, and he'd struck lucky. Rosalinde Fuller, a liberated modern girl, believed in having fun. She fancied Fitzgerald's blond looks and what she afterwards described as his 'gay challenging face'. He introduced himself, and immediately suggested they leave

| *Double portrait of Rosalinde Fuller by Francis Bruguière, late 1920s.*

the party. Outside the Plaza, he hired a hansom cab and told the driver to take them round Central Park. Some years later, Rosalinde wrote about what followed:

> …we got in, pulling the rough hairy rug round our legs. Scott shut the folding doors as though sealing an envelope… we seemed to have left the earth and were riding in a circuit of our delight… the clip-clop of the horse's hooves made a background to our discovery of each other's bodies. Eager hands feeling in warm secret places under the old rug, while the bouncing of the horse's bottom was our only contact with the outside world. 'You have Egyptian ears,' whispered Scott, 'and the look of a naughty boy.'

After that first night, the affair was full on. 'We made love everywhere', wrote Rosalinde, 'in theatre boxes, country fields, under the sun, moon and stars.' She was twenty-seven, sexually experienced and four years older than Fitzgerald, and within hours she had successfully demolished his sexual inhibitions. She had a talent for this, having previously cheered up an unhappily married brother-in-law. The relationship with Fitzgerald was short-lived and they didn't stay in touch, but they both remembered it for the rest of their lives. Fitzgerald mined his memories of Rosalinde in his writing over the years, on several occasions using cabs as the setting for romantic encounters – including a memorably chilly one in *The Great Gatsby* between Jordan Baker and the narrator, Nick Carraway. 'Our love affair lasted only a short time', wrote Rosalinde in her autobiography, 'but often in his stories I think I can see bits of myself dressed up in other situations.'

Although such brief flings were always on the cards, Rosalinde developed strong friendships with many of her lovers, having sex whenever they met, and corresponding regularly during relationships that often lasted for decades. Most revelled in her free-wheeling attitudes, accepting that marriage, or even faithfulness, was no part of her plan. When one lover she was fond of became tiresomely insistent on wedlock, the two of them consulted Bertrand Russell over dinner in Soho, Rosalinde rejoicing when the great philosopher endorsed her commitment to free love and told her companion to stop being a fool and take what the gods had given him.

Rosalinde had first gone to America in 1913 on the advice of the folksong expert Cecil Sharp. In a singing trio with her two younger sisters, they performed English folk songs to great acclaim, touring the country and finishing up with a performance at the White House for President Woodrow

Wilson. By 1919 she was in New York and trying to become a straight actress. At first she found it hard to escape revue, but picked up good work as lead singer in the highly popular *Greenwich Village Follies*. Then, in 1921, unknown as an actress, she was chosen by the actor John Barrymore to play Ophelia to his Hamlet on Broadway. American theatre-goers, tired of the stifling formalities of pre-war cultural life, were more than ready for something new and radical, and Barrymore – a superstar of stage and screen – gave it to them. He threw out all the reverence, the fustian and the traditional stage business usually attached to Shakespeare, and, in the words of one reviewer, 'almost single-handedly dragged the English-speaking world's understanding of the Bard into the modern age'. Critics and audiences went wild for a production that they felt caught the spirit of the times.

Little Rosalinde Fuller threw herself enthusiastically into this daring approach to theatre. Barrymore had been searching long and hard for his Ophelia, and he auditioned her just ten days before rehearsals began. 'Yesterday', he wrote in a letter to his wife, 'Miss Fuller who is a folk singer went through the part. She is a strange unprepossessing little English woman but has a detached rather zany quality… something very effective might be gotten there perhaps – particularly in the mad scenes.' How right he was.

Barrymore's vision for the play included a startlingly frank sexuality that unsettled some of his cast. He described the first court scene to his Gertrude, the American actress Blanche Yurka. 'It's a drunken orgy… court ladies loll with their shoulders and bosoms half bare… it's a sensuous, dissolute court, dominated by a lecherous King. In the midst of it Hamlet sits, a mute black figure, bathed in firelight.' Barrymore afterwards described his Hamlet as a normal, healthy, lusty young fellow designed to appeal to a younger audience, but perhaps even he was startled by Miss Fuller's enthusiastic response to his ideas. Her mad scenes were so lewd that several of her fellow actors found her performance bordering on the offensive. Barrymore, however, thought it wonderful; every night he left his dressing room to watch her from the wings. 'Her singing of the songs,' he said, 'would have melted the heart of God.'

Always on the look-out for a new lover, Rosalinde was more than up for some off-stage dalliance with Hollywood's greatest heart-throb. Often after the performance a small tie-on label marked 'Mr Barrymore' would be delivered to her dressing room as a coded invitation for her to pay him a visit. 'Then', she wrote afterwards, 'folded together on his sofa with his still-warm tights and tunics hanging against the wall, amidst the smell of powder and grease-paint, we would lose ourselves in a sort of mirage of love… and I would watch his beautiful face hanging over me…' At the end of the tour following their second season, Barrymore gave her a replica of the locket he had worn as Hamlet. Inside it was a folded paper on which he had typed the beginning of Hamlet's letter to Ophelia:

> 'Doubt that the stars are fire,
> Doubt that the sun doth move,
> Doubt truth to be a liar,
> But never doubt I love.'

The notoriety of her performance as Ophelia followed Rosalinde throughout her long life, eclipsing all other achievements in her stage career. 'Rosalinde Fuller, who played Ophelia to John Barrymore's celebrated Hamlet in 1922, has died in her sleep in London… she was 90 years old,' wrote her obituarist in the *New York Times* sixty years later.

Among those who found the performance and the actress unforgettable was American photographer Francis Bruguière, commissioned by *Harper's Bazaar* in 1921 to photograph Rosalinde as Ophelia. The pictures were the first of dozens he was to take of her over the next two decades. He photographed all of her and bits of her, clothed and unclothed, alone and with others. He had found his model and his muse and they were together until his death.

Rosalinde never forgot the first time Bruguière photographed her. 'He disappeared under a large piece of black velvet and looked through the lens straight into my heart'. Later, in his darkroom as the prints developed, came the first kiss. 'The red light and the acrid smell of the hypo enveloped me like an embrace, and a love affair that struck deeper than any of the others began.'

Bruguière was forty-eight years old when he and Rosalinde arrived in London from America in 1927. He brought with him a portfolio of extraordinarily inventive photographs of actors and stage designs as well as multiple exposures, surreal images and solarisation prints, all years ahead of Man Ray. He'd been photographing light and abstract forms from the early 1900s, and his first one-man show in New York had helped confirm the idea that photography could be seen as modern art. Acknowledged by fellow professionals during his lifetime as one of the great iconoclasts, Bruguière was completely indifferent to public recognition. He couldn't stand any kind of social or intellectual affectation, disdained the establishment, whether in art or society, and ran a mile from anything smacking of what he considered 'bourgeois acceptance'. A true original, he did what he did and let the world pass by on the other side. In 1949, four years after Bruguière's death, Cecil Beaton acknowledged his debt to this brilliant but curiously unsung artist:

The Photographer and his Muse

| *Francis Bruguière self-portrait, 1930.*

'There was something so self-effacing about Mr Bruguière himself that during his lifetime he was less acclaimed for the originality of his work than many of his disciples who achieved more notoriety than the master. Among those whom he encouraged and inspired at the beginning of their careers I should like to include myself.'

Bruguière came from a family of wealthy San Francisco bankers of French and Spanish origin. Educated on America's East Coast, he learnt to love music, painting and poetry during family holidays in Europe. In 1905 in New York, captivated by the camera, he fell in with leading pioneers of photography such as Frank Eugene and Alfred Stieglitz, who accepted him as a Fellow of the radical Photo Secession movement, which promoted photography as a fine art. By 1906 he was back in San Francisco and opening his first studio.

The family business collapsed at the end of the First World War, and in 1918 Bruguière, now married, returned with his wife and son to New York, where for the first time he was forced to rely on his photography to support them all. He found work for *Harper's Bazaar*, *Vogue*, *Vanity Fair* and the Theatre Guild, recording stage sets and models for New York's leading theatre producer-designers and taking portraits of the day's Broadway stars. Bruguière gave a modern twist to this conventional work, relishing sitters who were open to a more daring approach. 'Sometimes', he wrote, 'I find persons who, though they do not understand just what I am aiming for, are yet willing to experiment and will lend their time and energy to me.' Rosalinde Fuller, bold and unconventional, was truly after his own heart. He'd also come across a young German dancer called Sebastian Droste, an eccentric character who pretended to be a baron and was busy worming his way into the heart of New York society. Droste and Rosalinde became the inspiration and the two sole actors for a series of stills for Bruguière's fantastical film *The Way*. Droste died of a brain haemorrhage in 1925 and the film was abandoned, but the stills remain as some of the earliest surreal works by an American photographer.

Arriving in London in 1927, Bruguière began experimenting with a stream of new ideas, among them *Light*

The Photographer and his Muse

Courtesy of the George Eastman Museum

| Double print of Rosalinde Fuller, unclothed with cello, by Francis Bruguière, circa 1934.

Rhythms, the first British abstract film, made in cooperation with his great friend, the journalist and critic Oswell Blakeston. A hugely prolific writer of filmscripts, plays, novels, cookery and travel books, Blakeston had a quick eye for the bizarre and outrageous – a quality certain to appeal to Bruguière and Rosalinde – and a fancy for the Bohemian life. 'A friend of boozy poets, and me,' said Dylan Thomas. Blakeston became a regular visitor to Swan Court when, in 1932, Bruguière and Rosalinde moved into flat 101, just below McKnight Kauffer and Marion Dorn. Another chosen companion was Lance Sieveking, then the BBC's Assistant Director of Education and subsequently its drama script editor through the nineteen-forties. Rosalinde, a busy actress, would frequently return home after her evening's performance to find Kauffer, Marion Dorn, Sieveking, Blakeston and Bruguière deep in discussion, gin on the table, cats on the chairs.

Bruguière had always seen work in the commercial world as a new challenge for photography, and life in London offered plenty of enticing opportunities. Rosalinde's brother Walter Fuller, editor of *Radio Times* in the nineteen-twenties and a keen admirer of Bruguière's work, commissioned him and McKnight Kauffer to design a series of advertisements combining photographs, text and surreal imagery. The Charnaux Corset Company, Shell and the British Postal Service all commissioned ads using Bruguière's acclaimed cut-paper abstractions and light imagery. In 1937, with the architect Oliver Hill, he designed the entrance to the British Pavilion at the Paris Exposition, covering fifty-foot-high curved walls with photomurals of scenes from rural and industrial England. The plywood walls were painted with a light-sensitive plastic paint, onto which the photographs were enlarged, the first time this process had ever been used on such a scale.

Throughout the thirties, flat 101 became the background for the many experimental nude photographs Bruguière took of Rosalinde, often with others. When the American playwright Paul Osborn and his wife Florence were in London, Bruguière often photographed the three of them in the sitting room, tangled up naked together on the floor. Privacy was

(From left) Edward McKnight Kauffer, Rosalinde Fuller and Francis Bruguière in flat 101, Swan Court, 1935.

not always assured. During one Sunday evening session, the housekeeper, ignoring all the nudity on display, put her head round the door to ask when Madam would like coffee served. Another photograph from the Swan Court years shows the fully-dressed Rosalinde on a sofa with Bruguière himself and Kauffer in an uncomfortable-looking three-way hug. Behind the trio is a very familiar Critall window and tiled sill. Seeing Rosalinde so closely entwined with Kauffer raises a rather intriguing question: given her track record for cheering up men in difficult relationships, did she perhaps offer to console Kauffer on the occasions when he and Marion Dorn temporarily separated to rejuvenate their affair? Certainly her relationship with Bruguière was acknowledged to be open, although they remained devoted to each other until his death. He was the main point of her love life, she said, the others only shadows that floated across it. Often touring, she returned whenever she could to be with him, and at the beginning of the war, frightened that she would be unable to accompany Bruguière if he was sent back to America, she accepted when one of his obliging friends proposed marriage to get her an American passport. They quickly divorced when the friend met a girl he wanted to marry for real.

Rosalinde had made her London stage debut in 1927, and she worked constantly throughout the thirties, including in plays by Shaw and as a notable Irina in Chekhov's *Three Sisters*. By the end of the decade she was doing a stint as one of Sir Donald Wolfit's leading ladies at the Old Vic, employment which was not without some non-theatrical excitements. On September 1st 1939, two days before war was declared, Wolfit began rehearsals for a Shakespearean tour of provincial theatres with Rosalinde playing Viola, Katharina, Portia and Desdemona. It was the 'Phoney War'; fearing bombs, people were leaving London. There were rumours of all theatres being closed. The company's young male actors were on the immediate call-up list and the company manager jumped ship for Devon. Rosalinde, his leading lady, was in America but Wolfit pushed on, refusing to quit, and she proved just as intrepid. Facing the prospect of an Atlantic teeming with U-boats, she made two attempts to get home. Each time the liner turned back. At the third go she made it, and they opened in Brighton as scheduled. 'A brave deed', said Wolfit, and so it was: the liner *Athenia* was torpedoed on September 4th and a month later the steamer *Clement* followed.

In the autumn of 1940, with the Blitz well under way, Rosalinde joined Wolfit at the Strand Theatre in *Lunchtime Shakespeare*. The back of the theatre and the dressing rooms had been destroyed by a bomb, but they put on excerpts from the plays with songs and sonnets between one and two in the afternoon. They were paid just three guineas a week and the theatre lost money, but thousands of Londoners found solace in the words of Shakespeare during their lunch break. By the end of the year, six other theatres had followed suit.

By 1940, Bruguière's health was failing. He and Rosalinde gave up the Swan Court flat, and to escape the bombs he moved to the village of Middleton Cheney in Oxfordshire, the home of Rosalinde's sister Cynthia and her husband. On May 8th 1945, just as peace was declared, he died from bronchial complications resulting from the tuberculosis he'd had in his twenties. Rosalinde and Cynthia were at his bedside. Rosalinde gave a children's slide to the village playground in his memory. At the bottom of the slide a plaque read: 'This is a present to the children of Middleton Cheney from their friend Francis Bruguière of San Francisco'. Much mourned by his friends and the fellow professionals who acknowledged him as one of the great avant-garde photographers, Bruguière died largely unknown to the world. Many of his photographs, still startling and strangely affecting, can be seen in James Enyeart's definitive biography *Bruguière: his photographs and his life*.

In the nineteen-fifties, Rosalinde began writing a series of one-woman shows that she performed to acclaim around the world, including tours of the Middle East. In Belize, British Honduras, in 1964, she was cheered to the echo with a show lasting a full two hours and including excerpts from Nadine Gordimer's *Harry's Presence*, de Maupassant's *Window Game*, Chekhov's *Regrets* and Dickens' *David Copperfield*. Many of her tours were funded by the British Council and she received the OBE in 1966. Her last stage appearance was in Durban at the age of eighty-three, in an adaptation of the works of Katherine Mansfield.

When it came to her varied and energetic sex life, Rosalinde showed no signs of flagging as she grew older. In

Rosalinde Fuller in Temptations, *her adaptation of short stories by Anton Chekhov. Arts Theatre, London, 1969.*

her late sixties, after suffering a heart attack while on tour in the Middle East, she returned home and was advised to rest for two months. Was it all right, she asked her shocked English doctors, to start making love again? In moderation, they eventually advised – not a suggestion likely to appeal to, or even be understood by, Rosalinde, who at the time had two regular partners plus other lovers during her tours.

In March 1968 Rosalinde recorded Desert Island Discs with Roy Plomley. The recording has not survived, but we know her final choices. Her favourite track was *Je Ne Regrette Rien* by Edith Piaf and her chosen book, just blank pages and pencils. Her luxury was a full-length mirror. Did this totally uninhibited woman talk to Plomley about her lifelong addiction to free love, one wonders? And if so, did it make the final edit?

She died in London at the age of ninety, appearing, like Piaf, to carry no regrets into her old age: 'I have, all my life, lived very consciously in the present and the future and have hardly ever looked back.'

MAIN SOURCES

Barker, Clive and Gale, Maggie B (eds): *British Theatre Between the Wars*. Cambridge University Press, 2000.

Harwood, Ronald: *Sir Donald Wolfit: His Life and Work in the Unfashionable Theatre*. Secker and Warburg, 1971.

Mellow, James R: *Invented Lives: F. Scott and Zelda Fitzgerald*. Souvenir Press, 1985.

Morrison, Michael: *John Barrymore, Shakespearean Actor*. Cambridge University Press, 1997.

Winnington, Peter G (ed): *Kissing the Joy: The Autobiography of Rosalinde Fuller OBE*. Letterworth Press, 2018.

Winnington, Peter G: *Walter Fuller: The Man Who Had Ideas*. Letterworth Press, 2014.

The definitive book on Francis Bruguière and his work is Enyeart, James: *Bruguière: His Photographs and his Life*. Alfred Knopf, 1987.

6

A Double Life
Antony Gibbons Grinling MC
(1896-1982)
Flat 132 1932-1939

I FIRST LAID EYES ON A GIBBONS GRINLING sculpture in the summer of 2015 in the Wiltshire home of his daughter Amanda Relph. *Dancers* is a dramatic sixty-six-centimetre high piece made around 1929 in polished patinated brass on a marble base, featuring a naked dark-skinned man holding aloft a pale and pliant female figure. It's a sculpture that must have carried a certain ambiguity in an era when black musicians and dancers, exotic and sexually daring, were storming the theatres, cabarets and jazz clubs of London and Paris. There's an unmistakably erotic whiff of abduction in the pose as the black male figure, foot on the step, carries off his unresisting pale-skinned prize.

Dancers by Antony Gibbons Grinling, 1929.

Grinling, a dedicated although out-of-hours sculptor, chose a good time and place in which to follow his muse. 'Sculpture, which has been a moribund art in England for 400 years, is once more alive and vigorous', wrote critic Herbert Read in July 1933. The roll call of Grinling's famous contemporaries is impressive: Henry Moore, Barbara Hepworth, Jacob Epstein, Eric Gill, John Skeaping, Eric Kennington, Frank Dobson and so on. Five decades later, the Fine Art Society mounted an exhibition of the best of British sculpture from the inter-war years, and there, among these well-known luminaries, is Antony Gibbons Grinling. In the photograph chosen to

| Antony Gibbons Grinling in front of the Cambridge Theatre relief depicting dance, 1930.

introduce his entry in the exhibition catalogue we see him as he was in his Swan Court days – dark-haired, good-looking – posed in front of one of the bas-reliefs he was modelling for London's Cambridge Theatre in 1930, not long after completing *Dancers*. His clothes – surely chosen for the occasion – carry influences from his double life; immaculate office uniform of stiff white collar and tie underneath artist's overalls, right hand clutching sculptor's chisel and protective gloves. He's not too happy in front of the camera, the pose stiff, eyes slanting away from the lens. Over his shoulder the relief shows a voluptuous kneeling nude and her male partner, framed by a dancer's elongated legs and mimicking their creator's serious gaze.

The Cambridge Theatre, currently home to Andrew Lloyd-Webber's musical *Matilda*, sits between Mercer and Shelton Streets in Covent Garden's Seven Dials. Opened in 1930, it's a rare early example of a London theatre built in the moderne expressionist style pioneered in Germany in the previous decade. The Russian-born architect Serge Chermayeff was commissioned to design the interior and he turned to Grinling for some decorative touches. Following what was to become a lifelong fascination with the human form, Grinling took the themes of dance, music and drama for three bronze friezes featuring nude figures in bas-relief, one a lunette in the vestibule with two silver-leafed panels in the space beyond. Many of Chermayeff's original decorative features in the Cambridge have gone, but following restoration work in the eighties, you can see the beauty of Grinling's nudes today as they cavort elegantly above the hordes of harassed parents buying Matilda-logo-ed T-shirts in the foyer below.

Chermayeff, much sought after for the originality and perfection of his interior details, now turned his attention to

Studio (flat 132) designed by Serge Chermayeff for Antony Gibbons Grinling, with rug by Marion Dorn, 1933.

Grinling's new Swan Court studio. His design featured built-in cupboards and bookshelves in striped Australian walnut, incorporating an electric fire and huge mirror, the recesses painted a deep rose-pink. The windows were curtained in putty-coloured jute complementing one of Marion Dorn's rugs. The furniture included tubular steel dining-chairs and an armchair upholstered in zebra hide. With Grinling's sculptures on display as an integral part of the whole design, Chermayeff's shiny modern interior perfectly expressed the artistic side of his client's dual life.

Art had always been part of Grinling's world. His mother was a talented watercolourist who'd exhibited at the Royal Academy in the eighteen-nineties. He was sent to Harrow, where, like Chermayeff a few years later, he was taught by William Egerton Hine, one of the best public-school art masters of the period, whose students included Cecil Beaton and Victor Pasmore. Grinling won the school's Yeats Thompson Art Prize, as did his son later. This inspiring early start did not lead on to full-time study. He missed out on Cambridge when war came, and was commissioned into the Hertfordshire Regiment, winning a Military Cross before being badly gassed in the final Spring offensive of March 1918. Convalescence in Sicily gave him the chance to study carving and modelling with an Italian sculptor, rekindling his love of the arts.

Back in England in 1920, Grinling determined to carry on sculpting but felt it too late to go to university or art college. He followed his father into the family firm, distillers W&A Gilbey, and began the two very different lives that he maintained until his retirement from Gilbey's over four decades later.

Loving the modern in art, cars and clothes, Grinling also insisted that business should move with the times, his fellow directors often hard to convince when it came to anything new and different. In a bid to rid the company of elderly directors bent on vetoing progressive ideas, as Managing Director he insisted on compulsory retirement at sixty-five, a ruling he himself was the first to succumb to.

In the mid-thirties, Gilbey's decided to commission new offices to be built alongside the company's distillery and warehouses behind King's Cross Station. Grinling threw himself enthusiastically into the project, bent on shaking off his fellow directors' ideas of what constituted a suitable office building for an old-established firm. When he proposed Chermayeff as the architect, he was met with a storm of protest. The board, horrified at the prospect of employing a Modernist – and a foreigner to boot – only caved in when told that Chermayeff had been educated at Harrow.

It was a tricky commission. The site, overlooking the Regent's Canal between Oval Road and Jamestown Road, was bombarded by constant noise and vibration from trains in and out of King's Cross and iron-wheeled carts rumbling over granite setts. Chermayeff's answer was to float his reinforced concrete building on layers of cork, double-glaze the windows and install air-conditioning throughout. The lower floors were for wine storage and offices, with the top floor given over to the directors' suite, with boardroom, dining room, clubhouse and access to a terrace with wide views over London. Here the interior comfortably married the old and the new: you sat on modern Plan chairs under a wall of old company portraits and a huge antique tapestry. The result, said architectural historian Alan Powers, was 'a masculine modernism that could appeal to the non-aesthetic English gentleman, with its sense of quietly spoken quality and technical perfection, like a good yacht or car… unencumbered by fading symbols of class and nation'. Not so very far from Grinling's approach to sculpture, with its marriage of artistic expertise and a determined, if gentle, Modernism. He must have enjoyed this stimulating new workplace.

Today Gilbey's are long gone, and their site is now part of the bustling regeneration of the whole King's Cross area. After some sympathetic external renovation, the Grade 2 listed Gilbey House, home to several different companies, has been renamed Academic House. Today's Gilbey House is the old gin distillery next door, now converted into coveted flats overlooking the Regent's Canal.

Notwithstanding the daily grind of office life and a major building project, Grinling's sculpting flourished during his Swan Court years. He enjoyed London's go-ahead artistic circles, serving on the committee of the Twentieth Century

| Awakening *by Antony Gibbons Grinling. Figure of girl in Kauri pine, 1938.*

Group and enjoying the company of artists and architects such as Paul Nash, Jack Pritchard, Wells Coates and Raymond McGrath. No part-time dabbler, his output was astonishing for someone with a serious day job. Working mostly in stone and metal in the twenties, after he came to Swan Court he turned to wood. It was a material he loved, finding inspiration in its natural shapes and grains. 'Wood has nobility of form as well as the rhythm of growth', he wrote in an article for *Wood* magazine in 1936. 'It has life and dynamic, while stone is static and asleep'. His pieces, ranging from the abstract to the figurative, display a compelling combination of emotional charge and perfection of line. He had many commissions from the nineteen-twenties to the nineteen-sixties and exhibited at leading London art galleries and at the Royal Academy from 1946. His first one-man exhibition was at Tooth's in 1934. He also made garden statues for Queen Mary's Dolls' House and a room of tubular steel sculpture and furniture for Whiteley's department store. Today his work is mostly in private collections but can be seen at www.antonygibbonsgrinling.co.uk. You can't help but wonder what else this thoughtful, talented artist might have produced had he dedicated his whole life to the task.

Grinling left Swan Court at the beginning of the war when he was recalled to active service, rejoining his regiment in September 1939. Never fit since his gassing in 1918 and subject to severe bronchial attacks, he was invalided out of the army in May 1944. By the nineteen-sixties, severe sight loss from the long-term effects of mustard gas made sculpting impossible, but he turned to landscape painting after his retirement from Gilbey's in 1965. Shortly before suffering a stroke in 1977, he wrote the words that were quoted in his funeral elegy: 'Life is haphazard, and full of beauties which I try to catch as they pass.'

MAIN SOURCES

Conversations with Antony Gibbons Grinling's daughter Amanda Relph, his son Jasper Grinling and family papers.

Gibbons Grinling, Antony: 'Wood as a Sculptural Material' in *Wood Magazine*. June 1936.

The National Heritage listing for the Cambridge Theatre at www.historicengland.org.uk

Powers, Alan: *Serge Chermayeff: Designer, Architect, Teacher*. RIBA 2001.

Skipwith, Peyton: *Sculpture in Britain Between the Wars*. Fine Art Society 1986. This exhibition catalogue has a fine introductory essay by Benedict Read as well as biographical pieces and illustrations of work of the forty-six exhibited sculptors, including Antony Gibbons Grinling.

Website at www.antonygibbonsgrinling.co.uk

7

The Broken-Hearted Poet
*The Hon. Bryan Walter Guinness
(later 2nd Baron Moyne) (1905–1992)
Flat 143 1933-1940*

I N 1930, EVELYN WAUGH PUBLISHED HIS SECOND novel *Vile Bodies*, a book that was to become one of the most famous depictions of the roaring Twenties. It has a simple dedication: 'With love to Bryan and Diana Guinness'. In his travel book *Labels*, also published that year, Waugh uses the same dedication, adding 'without whose encouragement and hospitality this book would not have been finished'. The dedication has its ironic side. Waugh had written the book while in refuge with the recently married Guinnesses after his first wife Evelyn Gardner left him for her lover John Heygate. Two years later, Diana Guinness was also to run off in pursuit of another man, a reckless action that led directly to her heartbroken husband's arrival in Swan Court in 1933.

Growing up, the young Bryan Guinness had everything, from his enormous fortune to the romantic good looks that ran in the family. Hugely popular on the social circuit, the polio he'd contracted at Eton didn't prevent him becoming a first-class dancer; he could stop the conversation in a ballroom when he took to the floor, often partnered by his mother, Lady Evelyn Guinness, whom he adored. Up at Oxford, he dropped effortlessly into a coterie of golden and gifted young men that included Evelyn Waugh, Harold Acton, Robert Byron, John Sutro and Brian Howard, making lifelong friends who loved him for his endearingly sweet nature. He also regularly underspent his £6000 annual allowance, a habit so unusual in the circles he moved in that it caused his mother some concern.

| *Bryan Guinness. Drawing by Augustus John, 1933.*

Launched into London, Guinness began reading for the Bar. It's hard to believe that such a career could ever have suited him. He was sensitive and so shy that making a public speech could make him physically sick. But London also offered dances, and at one of them, in 1928, he met and fell for the eighteen-year-old Diana Mitford. A beauty and the third of the soon-to-be-notorious Mitford sisters, Diana was miserably bored with life at her family's country home in Oxfordshire. She loved books, music and gaiety, and a future surrounded by chickens, ponies and turbulent sisters was out of the question. Marriage was the escape route. What she saw in Guinness was not so much the man as his circle of brilliant friends. Talented and fun, they would draw her into the glamorous artistic set she dreamed of. When he proposed, her parents said she was too young, so she sulked through the summer of 1928 until reluctantly they gave in.

The engagement rang plenty of warning bells within their circle – if the two of them had been disposed to listen. Diana's eldest sister Nancy had many misgivings. 'The more I see of Bryan the more it amazes me that Diana should be in love with him, but I think he's quite amazingly nice', she wrote to her mother. Guinness himself could have heeded some indications that his feelings were not wholeheartedly reciprocated. Declaring passionately to Diana in a Hampstead garden that their love would last forever, his beloved replied dully, 'Well, for a long time anyway.' Hopelessly enamoured, he managed to convince himself that it was just another example of the Mitford family's love of teasing.

On January 30th 1929, a dazzling society wedding in St. Margaret's, Westminster, launched the two of them – propped up by a then enormous annual income of £20,000 – into London life among the so-called Bright Young People, a mix of blue-blooded socialites and the upper end of Bohemia.

| Bryan and Diana Guinness on honeymoon in Taormina, Sicily, in February 1929.

Jazzed up with an injection of glamorous low-lifes, the caperings of this exotic group caused a feeding frenzy in the gossip columns. Evelyn Waugh satirised their antics in *Vile Bodies* and many of them, such as Anthony Powell, Diana's sister Nancy Mitford, Cecil Beaton and John Betjeman, later became household names. Fun was the order of the day, and the respectability urged on them by their parents went out of the window. The most extreme parties were wild and eccentric, often with themes. The all-night Bath and Bottle party at St. George's Baths featured a special bathwater cocktail, Norman Hartnell gave a circus party and at art dealer Arthur Jeffries' Red and White party, the host wore white pyjamas with long white gloves festooned with ruby and diamond bracelets, his guests gorging for ten hours on lobsters and strawberries and smoking red and white cigarettes. Hoaxes were another fancy, elaborately planned, staged and designed to attract publicity. In his memoirs, written much later, Guinness shrugged off the idea that he and Diana had been part of this fast set. There was, he said, an immense difference between their group of talented friends and the sensation-mongering crowd so beloved of the gossip writers. With hindsight, he did concede that the distinction might be less evident to others than it was to him and Diana. Be that as it may, the Guinness' London home in a Lutyens house at 10 Buckingham Street, SW1, was the venue for many hectic parties, including one of the most notorious hoaxes of the age, cooked up by Guinness' old Oxford friend Brian Howard – an extravagantly camp dilettante whose mannerisms and turns of phrase were the inspiration for two of Evelyn Waugh's characters, Ambrose Silk in *Put Out More Flags* and the languid Anthony Blanche in *Brideshead Revisited*. Attractive to both women and men, with a graceful if minor literary talent, Howard, although known for his sharp wit and malicious tongue, was kind and loyal to his few great friends, like Guinness, who loved him. It was the attraction of opposites, wrote Howard's biographer, Guinness the serious, gentle dreamer and Howard the dynamic but doomed wrecker of lives, mostly his own.

Howard's greatest prank, the Bruno Hat art hoax, was planned with Evelyn Waugh and Guinness' brother-in-law Tom Mitford as an exhibition and party at the Guinness house. Years later, Diana said that the more they talked about it, the less enthusiastic her husband became. But he went along with it, and Howard got to work producing the pictures, skilful pastiches mostly painted on cork bathmats and framed in rope. Details of the exhibition were leaked to Lord Birkenhead's daughter Lady Eleanor Smith – herself a participant in many wild happenings – for her column in the *Sunday Dispatch*. 'What will be almost a cocktail party', she wrote, 'is the private view of the exhibition of paintings by Bruno Hat, a painter of German extraction whose work is of the abstract type, seemingly derivative from Picasso and Chirico.'

As with all the hoaxes, it's hard to tell just who was being fooled; many of the people at the party guessed what was afoot, and some of the most popular gossip columnists were themselves on the fringes of the Bright Young crowd. The whole thing was more of a charade than a hoax, said Guinness afterwards.

On Monday July 29th, eminent art critics and connoisseurs joined the Bright Young People at 10 Buckingham Street. Mr Bruno Hat, grumpy and taciturn, sat in a wheelchair smoking a cheroot and drinking iced coffee. This was Tom Mitford, complete with heavy German accent, false moustache and dark glasses. The following day, *The Daily Express* headlined its news story 'Amazing Hoax on Art Experts – Unknown Artist with False Moustache', before going on to reveal that the paintings were the work of Brian Howard.

Hoax or not, Diana Guinness thought the paintings that decorated her drawing room 'lovely, amusing and decorative', as did others. Lytton Strachey bought one, though possibly just to please Diana, whom he greatly admired. But for Guinness, the Bruno Hat affair was the beginning of the end of his dalliance with the Bright Young People. He was not the stuff of which party animals are made – too gentle, too cerebral, too contemplative by nature. But his adored Diana loved it all, and continued to fill their frenzied social life with parties – too many, said Guinness afterwards, his enormous bank balance failing to lessen his disapproval when the cook's bills came in. Meanwhile life continued in a golden whirl of cocktail parties, dances, theatre trips, concerts and country house visits. They bought the beautiful Biddesden House in Wiltshire, and filled it with friends and endless weekend gatherings. Everyone fell in love with Diana. She was intoxicated, and Guinness's increasing possessiveness was beginning to be tiresome. He craved more time for his writing and to be alone with his wife. A couplet in his poem *The Cocktail Party* makes his view of their social life quite clear:

> Here friendship founders in a sea of 'friends',
> And harsh-lipp'd bubbly cannot make amends.

Cracks were appearing in the marriage, the incompatibility obvious to Diana, if not to her husband. By now he'd given up the Bar, having discovered he was never going to get briefs because the Clerk of his Chambers considered him too rich to need the work. In the next years Diana gave birth to two sons, but by 1932 she was restless. One night at a dinner party she met her nemesis, the thirty-six-year-old Oswald Mosley, who'd held office in both the Conservative and the Labour governments and was now setting up the British Union of Fascists. Mosley was a serial womaniser whose wife had to endure his many affairs, including those with her two sisters and her stepmother. Compared to her gentle, devoted and somewhat unworldly husband, Diana found Mosley impossible to resist; he was charismatic, sexually experienced and rather brutally masculine. Besotted, she left her husband and set herself up in a flat where she could live freely as Mosley's mistress. This caused a serious scandal at a time when discreet adultery was tolerated but marriage-breaking was taboo.

The splitting-up of the golden Guinnesses, seldom out of the gossip columns since their wedding, was a sign of the times: jazz age mentality had succumbed to the preoccupations of a more sober and reflective decade. Guinness, devastated, escaped abroad to recover. Still fond of him, in his absence Diana took great pains to find him a new London home, enlisting the help of their mutual friends McKnight Kauffer and Marion Dorn, who suggested Swan Court's flat 143, the studio flat along the corridor from theirs. In 1933 Guinness became their neighbour, finding his new home a peaceful and restorative bolt-hole that lasted until the war. After moving in, he published his first novel, *Singing Out of Tune*, with a book jacket designed by Kauffer. Guinness liked the design, commenting that Kauffer had contrived to put a most pleasing appearance on his melancholy tale. The novel, which documents a failing marriage, was based on Evelyn Waugh's experience, but might just as well have been a lament for its author's own domestic tragedy. In these first years of separation, Guinness wrote Diana many letters from Swan Court, expressions of love and a yearning to re-create the past. She remained protective of him, even coming once to sit on his bed in the flat when he was enduring a bout of 'flu. Likewise, he rushed to her bedside when she landed in hospital after a car accident.

Happier times came, however, and on September 21st 1936, passers-by on the King's Road noticed a well-known face among the bridegrooms who paused that day for photographs on the Registry Office steps. Guinness and his Scottish bride Elisabeth Nelson followed their wedding with a small party for close friends and relations in what he called their eighth-floor 'eyrie' in Swan Court. The simple ceremony, he said, was much more to his liking than the pageantry of his first wedding to Diana. He and his new wife shared many interests, in particular the farm and Arabian horse stud they developed at Biddesden. They went on to have nine children, prompting the offspring of the first marriage to remark that if they didn't stop procreating, even the enormous Guinness fortune would run out.

A fluent French speaker, during the war Guinness served as a liaison officer with the French in Syria. He was in the region when his father, then minister resident in the Middle East, was assassinated by Jewish terrorists. On becoming the second Lord Moyne, Guinness inherited Knockmaroon, the family house overlooking the Liffey near Dublin. He was made vice-chairman of Arthur Guinness, Son & Co. in 1949.

Guinness wrote steadily throughout his life, receiving most recognition for his seven volumes of poetry, particularly *Under the Eyelid* (1935). His play, *The Fragrant Concubine*, was put on in the West End in 1938. After the war there were six children's books, five novels and five plays. *A Riverside Charade* was performed at the Abbey Theatre, Dublin, in 1954. There were also two collections of short stories and three volumes of memoirs. His work is imaginative and engaging, though often a little too sweet. Diana's daughter-in-law Charlotte Mosley commented that he'd be better known as a writer if he'd suppressed his natural kindliness and delicacy and put more of the ruthlessness of life into his work.

Guinness loved the arts and the company of artists. His homes were full of paintings and artefacts by friends, among them works by McKnight Kauffer and carpets by Marion Dorn. He was governor of the National Gallery of Ireland from 1955. He was worked hard in the House of Lords, managing to overcome his natural diffidence about making speeches. He died at Biddesden House on July 6th 1992. *On a Ledge*, his final collection of poems, was published posthumously the same year.

His poetry is not forgotten. *The Summer is Coming* was set to music by Herbert Howells in 1964 for the Cork International Festival. It's a beautiful setting for this tender evocation of an Irish summer. In March 2015, up the road from Swan Court in Holy Trinity Church, Sloane Street, it was performed as part of a concert celebrating the passing of the seasons.

MAIN SOURCES

de Courcy, Anne: *Diana Mosley*. Chatto & Windus, 2003 and essay on Diana Mosley in *The Oxford Dictionary of National Biography*, January 4th 2007.

Guinness, Bryan: *Dairy Not Kept*. Compton Press, 1975.

Guinness, Bryan: *Potpourri From the Thirties*. The Cygnet Press, 1982.

Lancaster, Marie-Jaqueline (ed): *Brian Howard: Portrait of a Failure*. Blond, 1968.

Mosley, Diana: *A Life of Contrasts*. Hamish Hamilton, 1977.

Pugh, Martin: *We Danced All Night: A Social History of Britain Between the Wars*. Bodley Head, 2008.

Taylor, DJ: *Bright Young People: The Rise and Fall of a Generation 1918–1940*. Vintage, 2008.

8

An Occasional Modernist
Francis Lorne (1889-1963)
Flat 144, 1931-1939

I N THE SPRING OF 2016, BROWSING ON THE SHELVES of the London Library, I came upon a recently published book on Modernist terraces. The cover showed a row of four houses, icing-sugar white, photographed in bright sunshine against a clear blue sky with the etched outlines of winter trees rising to the upper-floor windows. The street is Wells Rise, close to the Regent's Canal in St. John's Wood. The handsome white-rendered Modernist terrace brings dramatic light to the narrow street, which is half in deep shadow cast by nearby high-rise buildings.

The terrace was designed by architect Francis Lorne in 1934, following a commission from the Prince of Wales'

| 4–10 Wells Rise, St. John's Wood, London NW8, designed by Francis Lorne in 1934.

mistress, the racy socialite Freda Dudley Ward. Much taken with the suave and rather dashing Lorne, Mrs Dudley Ward was probably on the look-out for new interests when she became his patron in 1934, as the Prince had finally discarded her for Wallis Simpson. Freda Dudley Ward's second husband, the exotically named Pedro José Isidro Manuel Ricardo Monés, Marqués de Casa Maury, also commissioned a house from Lorne at 58 Hamilton Terrace, Maida Vale. The house was featured in the Ideal Home magazine in September 1938. The Marqués had previously used Lorne's architectural practice to build the Curzon cinema in Mayfair, with Lorne as designer. Such upper-crust connections were key to Lorne's flourishing inter-war career, and thanks to Freda Dudley Ward he pulled off an entrée into the Prince of Wales' circle, resulting in several prestigious commissions.

Lorne must have relished his new social milieu as his own origins were modest. He was born in Falkirk where his father was a master joiner. At twenty-six he was articled to a Falkirk architect and went on to work and study in Glasgow, London, New York and Paris. During the First World War he served with the Canadian Engineers, moving back to New York in the nineteen-twenties. After the Wall Street crash, Lorne's sister Helen, an astute and feisty girl working in London for Sir John Burnet and Partners, persuaded her brother to join her in a project to rejuvenate the somewhat old-fashioned firm.

Originally taken on as office manager on the strength of an earlier book he'd written on running an architectural practice, Lorne soon showed himself to be less than suited to such a subservient role. He was stylish, maybe even a little flashy, with more than a whiff of transatlantic dash about him. Described by a contemporary as slim and dapper, with beautifully tailored clothes and sleek black hair, he was also worldly-wise and penetratingly observant. In the office he could be sharp-tongued and even aggressive with staff, and not always as sensitive as he might have been to his senior colleagues, particularly when his eye for the main chance got the better of him. Once, when Burnet's partner Thomas Tait was out of the office, Lorne cheekily sold to a London dealer a sculpture that had been given to Tait by the sculptor, Sir William Reid Dick RA. Before Tait knew what had happened, the outraged Sir William spied his gift on sale in the dealer's gallery.

It's hard to imagine Lorne suffering too much from this kind of mistake. He oozed confidence and showed a grand disregard for business conventions, receiving clients in silk shirts worn without a jacket, a casual approach absolutely unheard of at the time. He ruthlessly pursued work and publicity. He ferreted out the owners of under-developed sites, persuaded them to sell and then set about finding clients for them. He slashed the number of staff in the office and recruited a new team of his own, largely

Francis Lorne, date unknown.

from America and the colonies. This politically radical, even communist-leaning, new blood effectively brought the old regime to an end, and with Tait and Lorne at the helm, the firm became the leading architectural practice of the thirties. Tait won the RIBA Gold Medal for the best building of 1933 with his design for the Royal Masonic Hospital at Ravenscourt Park and Lorne co-authored the book that became the architects' bible of the decade, *The Information Book of Sir John Burnet, Tait and Lorne*.

Opinions on Lorne's ability as an architect have varied. He has some admired public buildings to his credit, in particular the Hospital Chapel for St. Dunstan's in Rottingdean, Sussex, and Evelyn Court in Hackney, a block of 1125 flats completed in 1934 for the Four Percent Industrial Dwellings. But his real strength was as a well-connected and articulate spokesman for the practice, arguing that modern architecture would only mean something if it was seen as 'a practical building problem for our own country, our own people, our own climate and conditions of life. Most of us,' he said, echoing Le Corbusier, 'have realised the thrill which comes from boarding an ocean liner, or flying to France on one of the big imperial airways planes, or sitting at the wheel of a high-powered motor car. They are so eminently suitable for use and so attractively presented that they give us an emotional kick.' Good buildings, he said, should do the same.

In 1930, Sir John Burnet Tait and Lorne had been asked to undertake the interior design of 144 Swan Court, an eighth-floor studio in the north block. In November 1931, the

© Architecture Illustrated, November 1931, RIBA Collections

| Flat 144, with fixtures and fittings designed by Francis Lorne.

magazine *Architecture Illustrated* ran a series of photographs of the flat showing the fashionable built-in furniture and details of the woods, fabrics and other materials used. Lorne must have liked what he'd done as he moved in and stayed until 1941. He lived the life of a fashionable bachelor in Swan Court during the week, in later years spending his weekends at a house in Ascot, a smart establishment designed for entertaining his upper-crust clients.

By the end of the nineteen-thirties, Lorne also had a firm foothold in Johannesburg society through his work for the Oppenheimers and the Anglo-American Corporation, and after the end of the war he was commissioned to design the Corporation's new head offices in Johannesburg, alongside his original building at 44 Main Street. Lorne settled in South Africa, leaving his partnership with Tait and working in Johannesburg until 1954 when he and his wife moved to Salisbury, Rhodesia where he died in 1963.

MAIN SOURCES

Fox, Thomas N: Francis Lorne 1889-1963, *The Thirties Society Journal* No.6, 1987.

Francis Lorne biography report: *The Dictionary of Scottish Architects* 1660-1980.

Francis Lorne (obituary): *The Builder*, July 5th 1963.

Jensen, Finn: *Modernist Semis and Terraces in England*. Ashgate, 2012.

9

The Unlikely Couple
Ernest Gianello Milton (1890-1974)
Naomi Gwladys Royde-Smith
(1875-1964)
Flat 79 1932–1933;
Flat 140/142 1933-1935

N OT LONG BEFORE HE DIED IN 2014, SIR DONALD Sinden recalled an occasion at the Theatre Museum in Covent Garden when a number of famous Hamlets each gave a speech from the play. The best of the lot, Sir Donald told me, was Ernest Milton. 'His 'To be or not to be' was magical. That marvellous voice; the hairs stood up on the back of my head.'

Many others in the profession – Sir Alec Guinness for one – thought Milton's playing of Hamlet unrivalled by any that followed it. And if you want to know what Milton himself thought, you can go online and watch him in an hour-long BBC Monitor programme of 1963, discussing the ins and outs of playing the Prince of Denmark with a young, chain-smoking Peter O'Toole and a portly, middle-aged Orson Welles. The thirty-one-year-old O'Toole, about to open as Hamlet for Laurence Olivier in the National Theatre's inaugural production, is amusing to watch as he languidly keeps his end up against the two opinionated veterans.

One of the outstanding actors of his generation, Ernest Milton was never out of work on stage, screen or radio in a career lasting around fifty years. Starting out in New York, by 1918 he was in London, where he spent two decades with Lilian Baylis' Old Vic Shakespeare Company, appearing in numerous plays and in most of the major Shakespearian roles. His Shylock, Lear and Richard II were widely praised; Baylis thought his Hamlet outstanding and one of the chief turning points in the Old Vic's fortunes.

Milton's Jewish ancestry may have helped when he created one of his most popular characters, the rich young Jew Ferdinand de Levis in John Galsworthy's *Loyalties*, a controversial play about anti-Semitism. Many people, including the director Basil Dean, thought this the finest performance of his career. Among his other successes in London and on Broadway was a starring role as Rupert Cadell in the 1929 production of Patrick Hamilton's savage home-erotic play *Rope*. As for his work in films, two that bear the test of time are Dallas Bowers' curious puppet version of *Alice in Wonderland*, in which Milton voiced the White Rabbit and the Vice Chancellor, and Alexander Korda's *The Scarlet Pimpernel* with Leslie Howard and Merle Oberon. Milton – always good at playing sinister – is faultlessly greasy as Robespierre addressing an aristo awaiting execution: 'I send you people to the guillotine for the future happiness of the human race, but I don't allow torture!'

The Unlikely Couple

Ernest Milton as Rupert Cadell in Patrick Hamilton's play Rope, *Ambassadors Theatre, London, April 29th 1929.*

Off stage, Milton was a colourful character and fond of a glass or two. He was a hybrid in many senses and it was well known in the profession that he was homosexual. Born in San Francisco, of Italian-American parents with Jewish ancestry, he subsequently became a Roman Catholic. Put up for the Garrick Club, to which many of his professional colleagues belonged, he was blackballed. Reasons are never given, but a present-day member suggested it was perhaps because he was a touch 'too flamboyant'. Interpret that how you will.

Very much an actors' actor, Milton was much relished by his colleagues for his eccentric over-the-top persona. Theatrical veterans still tell Milton anecdotes, many involving his legendary and long-running rivalry with actor-manager

Sir Donald Wolfit, a notorious up-stager and hard to work with. Milton too had a secure sense of his own importance. When they toured together, their two dressing-rooms would be labelled '1' and 'A' so that neither could say his was inferior. When Milton reluctantly agreed to play a Jesuit priest opposite Wolfit in the West End production of *The Strong Are Lonely*, the critic Kenneth Tynan commented that he would long recall these two expert players stealthily up-staging each other for the greater glory of God. John Gielgud remembered spying Milton across Leicester Square and shouting out, 'Hello, Ernest!' Back came the response, with a grand gesture and vibrato worthy of a Kean or an Irving, 'Who calls?' In Swan Court, one can imagine the spectacular echo that must have drifted up to the top floors when he greeted neighbours across the courtyard.

This was Ernest Milton in his heyday, an age when a beautiful voice and mannered theatrical gestures were part of a great actor's stock-in-trade, but even then he was not always to everyone's taste. You either found his performances mesmerising and unforgettable, or you thought him over the top, the latter a view we might share today. He certainly divided opinion at the time, attracting the same kind of contradictory criticism as his great Victorian predecessor Henry Irving. When he appeared in August 1926 at the Everyman Theatre in *A Balcony* – a play written by his future wife – *The Spectator's* critic called him 'the most naturally unnatural and sincerely artificial actor whom I can remember to have seen since the days of Sir Henry Irving'. In his Swan Court days he was riding high, but in the post-war world his style rapidly became out of date and by the mid-fifties he was having trouble with his lines.

The actress Ellen Sheean knew him in his later years when she was very young: 'He was a strange ambivalent character with a wonderful aura and a great voice, but it was a sad time as he couldn't get around the script. The management had doubts and made it impossible for him to continue. I know he was very bitter.'

Milton and the handsome, plump, chain-smoking Naomi Royde-Smith had been married for six years when they arrived in Swan Court. She was fifty-seven, trailing a long and distinguished career in the literary world and possessed of a forceful personality, a sharp wit and a sharper tongue. We get an earlier glimpse of her in 1921, when Virginia Woolf paid a visit to her home at 44 Princes' Gardens in Kensington, a popular salon where you could meet everyone in the literary world, the established and the up-and-coming.

| *Naomi Royde-Smith in 1932, by Elwin Neame Ltd.*

The gatherings were presided over by the forty-six-year-old Naomi, described by Woolf that night in her diary as 'dressed à la 1860, swinging earrings, skirt in balloons… she sat in complete command. Here she had her world round her. It was a queer mixture of the intelligent and the respectable'. Naomi basked in the company of literary luminaries such as Arnold Bennett, Edith Sitwell and WB Yeats, all frequent visitors to the gatherings she often jointly hosted with her friend and flatmate, the novelist Rose Macaulay. Macaulay later satirised Naomi as fashionable gossip Aunt Evelyn in her 1926 novel *Crewe Train*.

Born in Yorkshire and educated in London and Geneva, Naomi had moved to Chelsea in 1904, taking rooms in Oakley Street with her sister Leslie. Here she first tasted the joys of being a hostess, with journalists and writers welcome each Thursday evening for an 'At Home'. Both sisters found work at the *Westminster Gazette*, a Liberal evening paper published in London between 1893 and 1928 for the members of London's gentlemen's clubs. It was highly influential in British politics, despite a tiny readership of around a thousand.

Starting off on the *Gazette's* Problems and Prizes page, Naomi shot to journalistic stardom when she was made Literary Editor of the *Saturday Westminster Gazette*, the paper's weekend supplement. This was a significant coup. In her late thirties, beautiful, extremely well-read and more than up to competing with men on their own terms, she became the first woman in the country to reach such heights at a time when all influential jobs in journalism were held by men. She had great literary flair and soon the *Gazette's* reviews and articles became as highly regarded as those in the *Times Literary Supplement*. Distinguished poets competed each week in the competitions she set. Excited by the avant-garde in literature, over the next ten years she promoted and published the early work of many young writers, including Rupert Brooke, DH Lawrence, Graham Greene and T.S. Eliot.

In 1922 she left the *Westminster Gazette* to devote her time to writing books, perhaps less her forte than literary journalism. Immensely productive, over the next four decades she wrote several biographies, four plays and some forty novels of varying quality. In a time hostile to the exploration of sexuality, she wrote bravely about the lives of women loving women, men loving men, and tales about ordinary men and women, in love or not. Two of her first novels, *The Tortoise-Shell Cat* and *The Island*, deal openly with lesbian themes. *The Tortoise-Shell Cat* – held to be her best book and in and out of print since 1925 – centres on a thwarted relationship between a young teacher and a predatory older woman.

By 1926 she'd largely given up her frenzied social life, although she continued to review and was for a while art critic of *Queen Magazine*. In 1928 she published *The Weekend Book*, which included her well-known couplet – often attributed wrongly to Hilaire Belloc: 'I know two things about the horse, and one of them is rather coarse'.

Alongside her taste for literary lions, gossip and Modernist writing, Naomi had pursued a rich and varied sentimental life. In the spring of 1911 the poet Walter de la Mare, married and a keen family man, fell crazily in love with her. She published his work in the *Saturday Westminster Gazette* and as soon as they met, he was bewitched. Over the next years he wrote her around four hundred letters. He had no intention of leaving his wife and was by all accounts not much interested in sex. The relationship was intense and passionate, but in old age Naomi insisted that it was never consummated. The affair was known to de la Mare's wife Elfie, and although the emotional strain on all three was intense, de la Mare produced much of his best poetry during these years. This must have pleased

Naomi, who was much keener on being an artist's muse than on steamy affairs. Despite its stresses, the arrangement may have suited her; she was always sexually ambivalent towards the opposite sex but wanted those she loved to be men of genius. During the same period she also had a close romantic friendship with Rose Macaulay, who had been a tomboy as a child and believed she would grow up to be a man.

Naomi's marriage to Ernest Milton in 1926 seems on the face of it somewhat surprising, but perhaps she enjoyed stirring the confused sexual pot. In an intriguing link – probably brokered by her – between the two most significant men in her life, Ernest Milton's play *Christopher Marlowe*, published before their marriage in 1924, features a prologue in verse by Walter de la Mare. Added to Mr and Mrs Milton's conflicted sexual histories, there was also a big age gap, Naomi being fifteen years older than her bridegroom – though claiming to only twelve. However, there were compatibilities. She'd been dramatic critic of the *Saturday Westminster Gazette* for a while and had admired his acting before they met. She enjoyed the world of the theatre and had written an excellent biography of Mrs Siddons. Ernest Milton was a man of wide culture and sharp intelligence, likely to provide his new wife with the good conversation she relished. He was also a competent writer, whose novel *To Kiss the Crocodile* has surely autobiographical overtones. The hero is trying to find himself in a new world peopled with beautiful and rather camp young men, but on his deathbed he thinks only of a girl he realises he has loved all the time. Long out of print, a first edition now fetches around £350.

Whatever form the relationship took, the union was by all accounts happy and companionable, lasting until Naomi's death in 1964. De la Mare's biographer Theresa Whistler describes the marriage as 'long and successful, oddly assorted in some respects but devoted, even particularly touching – a triumph over unlikeliness by the strong-minded romantic woman that she was, and the histrionic, highly-strung, generous-minded actor. He placed her, for life, on a pedestal of admiration, though not by temperament drawn to her sex'.

In 1933 the Miltons moved from flat 79 to 140/142, the eighth-floor double studio on the north-eastern corner of the

Ernest Milton as the Mock Emperor in his adaptation of Pirendello's *Henry IV* at the Queen's Theatre, London, 1929. Costume by Marion Dorn.

north block, diagonally opposite that of McKnight Kauffer and Marion Dorn. They'd known each other since 1929 when Kauffer had designed the sets, and Dorn the fabrics, for Milton's play *The Mock Emperor*, an adaptation of Pirandello's *Enrico IV*. During his first months in Swan Court, Milton was managing the St. James' Theatre, where he was blacking up each night as Othello in a production with sets and principal costumes commissioned from Kauffer. The production failed, with Milton widely regarded as miscast, but Kauffer's set designs were much admired. Maybe this uneven verdict caused some embarrassment when the two of them passed the time of day in the courtyard, but at least Kauffer's sets weren't wasted: Milton gave them to the Old Vic where they were reused in the 1934–5 season.

Milton's time at St. James' was short-lived, management hardly his strong suit. *Othello* was followed by a production of *The Merchant of Venice* – also with Kauffer's sets – a production that must have caused Milton more frustration. The critics raved about his Shylock, but box office receipts were poor and the play closed after three weeks. However, he was always in demand for stage and screen work throughout his time in Swan Court, and in 1938 – perhaps watched by some of his neighbours in the block – he played the title role in a modern dress *Julius Caesar*, the first full-length production of a Shakespeare play on British television.

As for Naomi, life and work in Swan Court suited her muse. Perched up in her eighth-floor eyrie, ignoring the spectacular views over London to the north and east, she kept the typewriter going day and night. She'd published eight books since her marriage in 1926, of which the last, *The Delicate Situation*, was one of her better efforts. *The Bridge* appeared in 1932, followed two years later by *The Queen's Wigs*. *Jake* was published in 1935.

After the Miltons left Swan Court, they moved out of London, living in Winchester for several years during and after the war before ending up in a hotel in Hampstead. Naomi continued writing, publishing her last book in 1960. Described by her family as chain-smoking, un-corseted, and hugely amusing to the end, she died in 1964.

After Naomi's death, Milton became querulous and he alienated many people. Always prone to extravagant reactions, at the end of his life he felt he'd never received the accolades that were his due. In 1966 he turned down the offer of an OBE, perhaps seeing it as an insult compared to the knighthood he craved. He spent his last years in Denville Hall, the retired actors' home in north London. Largely neglected by the acting fraternity, he died there in 1974. Sir Alec Guinness, a close friend and fellow Roman Catholic, was one of the very few who attended his Requiem Mass.

MAIN SOURCES

Conversation with Sir Donald Sinden, December 22nd 2013.
Correspondence with Ellan Sheean, July 2013.
The BBC Monitor programme, originally screened on October 27th 1963.
Theatre review: *The Spectator*, September 4th 1926.
Barranger, Milly S: *Margaret Webster: A Life in the Theater*. University of Michigan Press, 2004.
Benton, Jill: *Avenging Muse: Naomi Royde-Smith 1875–1964*. Xlibris, 2015.
Guinness, Sir Alec: *Blessings in Disguise*. Hamish Hamilton, 1985.
Whistler, Theresa: *The Imagination of the Heart: The Life of Walter de la Mare*. Duckworth, 1993.
Virginia Woolf's diary entry for June 5th 1921. Woolf, Virginia: *Diaries*. Hogarth Press, 1978.

10

The Saucy Ingénue
Nancy O'Neil (1907-1995)
Flat 34 1935-1939

The marriage has been arranged and will take place, very quietly, between Dermot George Crosbie Trench of 41 First Street SW3 and Nancy O'Neil of 34 Swan Court SW3.

THIS PERSONAL ADVERTISEMENT FROM *THE Times* of May 31st 1938 catches the eye, the name Nancy O'Neil faintly improbable. And so it turns out. She was born Nancy Muriel Smith in Sydney, Australia, in 1907 and stage-struck from the word go. At eighteen – pert, pretty and not much over five feet tall – she came winging to London to study at the Royal Academy of Dramatic Art and lose her Aussie accent. She got her first stage engagement with Barry O'Brien's repertory company in Salisbury and then

Nancy O'Neil, publicity image, 1930s.

returned to Australia to tour in the play *Doctor Pygmalion*, a spin-off from the George Bernard Shaw classic.

Back in London, she got her first break into movies, becoming, as her obituarist put it decades later, one of many delightful ingénues who decorated British films in the nineteen-thirties. She played the Admiral's winsome daughter who is saved by Jack Hulbert from Chinese pirates in *Jack Ahoy!*, then joined another top musical comedy star of the

| Nancy O'Neil with Jack Buchanan in Brewster's Millions, 1935.

day, Jack Buchanan, in Herbert Wilcox's *Brewster's Millions*. She made endless 'quota quickies', the low-budget supporting pictures made under the Quota Act that forced the big American distributors to show a quota of British-made films. She was with Claude Hulbert in *Hello Sweetheart* in 1935, then *The Brown Wallet* – directed by the not-yet-famous Michael Powell – and *Head Office* in 1937, all for Warner's. Then there was *Fifty Shilling Boxer* (1937), *East of Ludgate Hill* (1937), *There Was A Young Man* (1937), *Darts Are Trumps* (1938)… the list goes on and on, at least thirty films. She was always working, skipping out from flat 34 day after day, off to Pinewood or Ealing Studios. There was always another movie to make, another script in her bag. Times were bleak; people couldn't get enough of these cheap and cheerful 'flicks' to lighten the national mood.

Nancy also saw opportunities in magazine advertising, becoming one of the first film stars to endorse expensive products, from fur coats to luxury cars. Her public loved the innuendo in captions such as 'Little Nancy O'Neil Will Ride in Nothing but a Big Cadillac!'

Then in 1938 she gave it all up and opted for marriage. She was into her thirties, getting a bit old to be an ingénue, and war was in the air. Her husband-to-be was a chartered accountant, and marriage probably seemed a safe port in the coming storm. They left for the country and had two children but she couldn't stay away from the business forever. After the war she came back in small supporting roles in films and television. In 1953 she played Mrs Blakeworth, the Town Clerk's wife, in the hugely successful Ealing comedy *The Titfield Thunderbolt*, with, among others, Stanley Holloway, Naunton Wayne and Sid James. She played her last role, a cameo with Vivienne Merchant, in a television play in the nineteen-sixties. She died in London in 1995.

MAIN SOURCES

Obituary in *The Independent*, March 17th 1995.

11
Wooing Chaplin's Girl
Virginia Cherrill (1908-1996)
George Francis Child-Villiers,
9th Earl of Jersey (1910-1998)
Flat 28 1934-1938

One Friday night in October 1928, the film world's great and good gathered at the Hollywood Legion Stadium to watch the boxing and wind down for the weekend. Among the spectators that night was Joe Adler, a hugely rich and sociable elderly man with top-notch connections throughout the film business. The partly paralysed Adler was pushed in his wheelchair by a startlingly pretty girl, the runaway teenage wife of his nephew Irving. Virginia Cherrill, recently arrived from Chicago at Adler's invitation, was just finding her feet in smart Hollywood circles. Very short-sighted, that night she'd forgotten her glasses and had to screw up her eyes to catch the action when the first fight began. She didn't take much notice of the wiry little white-haired man in tennis shorts in the next seat, watching her intently. When he leaned over and offered her a part in his latest film, she knew what he was after; she'd been warned by her new friends about overtures of this kind in Hollywood and she immediately moved to another seat.

'You didn't recognise Charlie Chaplin?' said the astonished Adler at the end of the fight. No, she said. To her, Chaplin was a skinny little guy with black hair and a moustache. Adler told her she must be mad; there couldn't be another girl in Hollywood who'd refuse an offer like that, made to a complete unknown and with no screen test required. He set about repairing the damage and got them invited to Chaplin's house for lunch the next day. Virginia wasn't keen; she'd come to Hollywood to forget her marriage, find new friends and have fun. She had no fancy to be a film actress.

Remembering the lunch decades later, Virginia recalled Chaplin's offhand manners, and the terrible pay he offered – just seventy-five dollars a week – but Joe Adler wouldn't let her argue. Chaplin gave her a date to sign the contract, and the deal was done. Virginia's poor start with her co-star was the precursor to a tetchy working relationship. They didn't like each other, and she's gone down in history as the only one of Chaplin's leading ladies that he neither married nor bedded.

In his autobiography, Chaplin's account of their first meetings was rather different from Virginia's, but the two of them certainly agreed about their on-set antipathy. He was approaching forty when he cast this unknown girl with no film experience to play opposite him in the silent film *City Lights*. He was at a tricky moment in his career. He'd been internationally famous by the time he was twenty-seven, and – until overtaken by Mary Pickford – the highest-paid artist in the world. Now his private life was shot to bits by a series of sexual and financial scandals, and when the Revenue sued him for $1.6 million in unpaid taxes, his hair turned white overnight. In January 1927 he had a nervous breakdown. Added to this, it was a bad time for a master of mime. The talkies had arrived; the writing was on the wall for silent films.

City Lights is set in London and tells the story of a blind flower-girl who develops a touching relationship with Chaplin's famous character, the Tramp. Chaplin had been searching for someone to play his blind romantic lead, and he knew he'd found her that night as he watched the ravishing girl in the next seat peering shortsightedly at the prizefighters. Then, on January 29th 1929, his find arrived for her first day's filming. She knew nothing about acting, nothing about making movies and nothing about Chaplin's working methods. She never

| *Virginia Cherrill as the blind flower girl in Chaplin's* City Lights, *1931.*

imagined she'd be in front of the camera on her very first day, but Chaplin wanted her in costume at once and on the set. He then proceeded to perform not only his part, but hers too. He acted out every single glance, every movement, just as he wanted it played, she said later. 'You found yourself thinking that he was you and that he was also the person he wanted you to be. It wasn't easy.' Four days later they were still filming the same tiny scene, the flower-girl's first meeting with the Tramp. It's a silent movie, she cheekily reminded Chaplin. Did it really matter how she mouthed 'Flower, Sir?' when nobody could hear her speak? 'Just do as I ask. Is it really so difficult?' he snapped. Weeks later, after a record three hundred and forty-two takes, Chaplin was at last satisfied, but the making of the movie continued to be a bumpy ride. At one point he even fired his naïve young co-star. When he couldn't find a replacement, he had to beg her to come back, grudgingly agreeing to increase her pay.

Towards the end of his life, Chaplin admitted to an interviewer that he had worked himself into a frenzy in his obsessive search for perfection with *City Lights*. He couldn't afford a failure, and he was working with a girl he dismissed as a useless amateur, a socialite, whose mind was always elsewhere. This may have been true; Virginia was much taken up with her social life, dining, dancing and dallying with a string of attractive men. But whatever the problems along the way, *City Lights* is right up there among Chaplin's all-time greats. It shows all the different sides of his genius – slapstick, pathos, pantomime and melodrama. It shattered audiences in 1931, and its appeal endures; the final scene where the flower-girl recognises the Tramp as her benefactor has passed into film legend as one of the most moving moments ever seen on screen.

City Lights made Virginia Cherrill an instant star and one of the most feted young women in Hollywood. Under contract to Fox, with a face the camera loved but no real acting talent, she made a handful of forgettable films. Her romantic life prospered in a string of minor affairs until one day she met a young English ex-vaudeville performer trying his luck in Hollywood. Born Archie Leach in a modest house in Bristol, he was now under contract to Paramount, who'd insisted on a change of name. As Cary Grant, he went on to captivate women all over the world. Virginia fell madly in love.

In her eighties, she told her life story to a friend who secretly recorded it. The tapes, which form the basis of Miranda Seymour's biography *Chaplin's Girl*, sparkle with wit, intelligence and a love of fun. This was a woman who prized, above all, people who could make her laugh. Cary Grant, master of mimicry, was a wit and he loved to tell jokes. His seriousness on screen was all a pose, she said. 'I never knew a man who could laugh so much, just giggling until the tears ran down his face. He'd tell stories in every kind of dialect and we'd both be laughing so much we couldn't speak.'

Sadly, the man who was to become one of Hollywood's great matinée idols was insecure, possessive and prone to jealous rages. Every so often Virginia had to escape, fleeing first to New York and then to England. Grant followed her. She told English friends that she was crazy with love for him but scared of the way he behaved. He was desperate to marry her; she prevaricated. Then, after discovering that the mother he thought had died years before was alive and in an asylum, he landed in hospital with a breakdown. His soft-hearted beloved gave in, and on February 9th 1934 they married in Caxton Hall and made plans for an immediate return to Hollywood, crossing the Atlantic free of charge with Cunard. The company got its money's worth thirty years later when it used an on-board photograph of the honeymooners to publicise the delights of the *QE2*. By this time, Cary Grant was one of the biggest all-time stars in the world, while his bride had slipped into near-obscurity.

The disintegration of Virginia Cherrill's marriage to Cary Grant is a depressing story of Grant's increasingly obsessive jealousy, alcoholism and occasional violence. The divorce case fuelled the gossip columns, Virginia's lawyer stating that Grant drank, beat his wife and had threatened to kill her. Older, more scandalous, rumours about Grant and his former housemate Randolph Scott surfaced again. On Christmas Eve 1934, after less than a year, the marriage was over.

The mid-thirties was a good time for a glamorous party-loving American girl to arrive in England. The post-war

| *Virginia Cherrill by Dorothy Wilding, 1937.*

changes had blown a broadside in the fortress of English upper-class life and, through her friend Edwina Mountbatten, the little girl from an Illinois farm was soon embedded in the highest of high society. Still hankering hopelessly for Grant, she fell into a romantic liaison with the twenty-three-year-old Maharajah of Jaipur. Jai, as he was known, was one of the finest polo players in the world and a regular on the English party circuit. Handsome, amusing and immensely rich, he escorted her everywhere that summer, dining and dancing at the Savoy, shopping at Aspreys, watching polo at Windsor and Cowdray and drifting off with her to Paris and Le Touquet. She adored him, she said, but he wasn't Cary.

One afternoon in the spring of 1935, Virginia and a friend, Robin Filmer-Wilson, drove out from her new flat in Swan

| *George Francis Childe-Villiers, 9th Earl of Jersey 1930*

Court to Hounslow. They wanted to take a look at Osterley Park, the eighteenth-century Adam house that belonged to the twenty-five-year-old Earl of Jersey. It was well-known that the Earl and his beautiful Australian wife Pat were hardly ever there, preferring their other home at Middleton Park in Oxfordshire. Virginia and Filmer-Wilson were wandering around the grounds when, to their embarrassment, the Earl appeared on the front steps. Apologies for trespassing were cut short with an immediate invitation to tea.

It was a curious party. Pat Jersey was away and her husband didn't seem to know where she was. The young Earl and his dog appeared to be the only residents. He was isolated and lonely, thought Virginia, in his gilded mausoleum of a house. But the tea went well, and plans were made to meet again. One curious outcome of the occasion occurred some time later, when eligible bachelor-about-town Filmer-Wilson had an affair with, and subsequently married, his host's absent wife.

Whatever Virginia privately thought of her host at this first meeting, it certainly wasn't as a lover. George Child-Villiers, 9th Earl of Jersey, was hardly a romantic match compared with Cary Grant or the glamorous Maharajah. Known from his Eton schooldays as Grandy – his courtesy title was Viscount Grandison – this remote and rather chilly young aristocrat had little in common with Virginia apart from their mutual love of dogs, but there was a more intriguing bond. Virginia loved art and had been encouraged in her interest by her close friend, the film actor Edward G Robinson, a serious buyer who'd put together a very fine collection of pictures. He introduced Virginia to his favourite gallery, the Lefevre in Mayfair. His relationship with the gallery was close, but he'd had to persuade them to take him seriously – in his memoirs, Robinson recalls with amusement the horrified looks from the gallery staff when they first saw a well-known Hollywood gangster walking through the door. Now, when Grandy Jersey told Virginia he wanted to start an art collection, she suggested he should buy the French Impressionists and took him to the Lefevre, kickstarting what was to become the young earl's lifelong passion.

Virginia was tepid about the Earl, but he knew he'd met the woman he wanted to marry. On April 14th 1936, a carefully staged scene of adultery took place in 28 Swan Court. The Earl of Jersey was 'discovered' in bed with a Canadian dancer called Olive Cliveden, who'd happily accepted a small fee for this service to a man with whom she'd previously had a brief affair.

Grandy Jersey's upbringing had more than a whiff of Hamlet about it. Taken away from Eton at thirteen with medical problems, he'd been schooled at home. In 1925, when her delicate son was fifteen, his recently widowed mother shocked the family by marrying the boy's tutor Ronnie Slessor – aged twenty-five and ten years her junior – who became master of the family homes at Middleton and Osterley. Grandy felt deeply betrayed by the young tutor he'd been closely attached to, but he bided his time until he was twenty-one, and then, with legal control of his inheritance, he removed his mother, her young husband and their two children from Middleton and withdrew his financial support. When his stepfather gave him an Alsatian puppy, he named it Claudius.

Virginia spent the summer of 1936 weighing up the merits of her two suitors. Grandy Jersey was grooming her to be his next Countess, but now the dashing Maharajah proposed marriage. They were an odd couple, Grandy a cold fish, Virginia said later, and the absolute opposite of Jai. After a visit to Jaipur – accompanied by the rather jealous Grandy, who'd invited himself along – the reality of life in India for

Maharajahs' wives was brought home to her. Purdah didn't appeal. She told Jai she wouldn't marry him but was happy to continue their relationship.

Back from India, Virginia was summoned down to 28 Swan Court where she found Grandy in bed, yellow in the face from a severe attack of jaundice. 'Are you going to marry Jai?' he demanded. 'No,' she said, 'I couldn't stand it.' The Earl then gave her a diamond ring and told her he'd written to ask her mother over from America for the wedding. After more months of prevarication, Virginia gave in, and on July 30th 1937, the Earl and his future Countess crossed the road from Swan Court to the Chelsea Registry Office and did the deed. Grander celebrations followed at Osterley.

It's hard to fathom why this beautiful fun-loving young woman – who could have had almost any man she wanted – should have chosen to marry Grandy Jersey, for whom she had no particular feeling. Did she do it for his matchless houses, his nine and a half thousand acres and the fact that he was one of the richest men in England? She seemed to have no great opinion of the English aristocracy in general. They have separate beds, she commented later, and the dogs always come first. But perhaps she married him to please her mother, smug as a cat with the cream in the Osterley wedding photographs. Whatever the reason, Virginia said yes, while telling Grandy firmly that she didn't love him. He wasn't worried; he wanted a wife and they did a deal – she could do what she liked so long as she was discreet. Sex was never part of the agreement, she said later. 'I paid him a visit from time to time.' No doubt the planning of private dates was made easier by the separate telephone line that Virginia had installed at flat 28, put in, oddly, under the name of Mrs V Cherrill Grant. 'I'm an American,' said Virginia. 'I love to telephone.'

In the event, while enjoying plenty of extra-marital flirtations, Virginia seems to have lived up to her side of the bargain, graciously playing the Countess when required, taking an interest in the Jersey estates, attending charity events and putting her talent for interior decorating to good use in the refurbishment of Middleton Park and Osterley. She failed in her attempts to give Grandy Jersey an heir, suffering at least two miscarriages. The Maharajah remained on the scene, wining and dining her in London and, within a year of her wedding, whisking her off on a very public holiday.

It's amusing to imagine the new Countess, sporting the latest chic Paris outfit with perfect hair-do and tiny hat, stepping out of her front door under Swan Court's eastern arch and getting blown to bits by the wind that so often funnels through from Chelsea Manor Street. When she was first in Swan Court in the summer of 1934 – her actual flat number then remains obscure – neighbours were electrified one day to find an enormous scarlet Bentley with white leather seats parked in the courtyard. This was a thank-you present, chauffeur included, from Max Ausnit, a Romanian steel magnate for whom she'd organised a dance for five hundred people. She thought the car would make her look like a kept woman and sent it back. 'Can you imagine how vulgar it was?' she said later. Its replacement, dark green with pigskin seats and gold fittings, seems to have been more acceptable. By the time she was twenty-eight, with her Hollywood fame augmented by elevation to the aristocracy, the press had a field day, her social junketing splashed all over the gossip columns and no doubt causing much interest to her neighbours in the block.

Just before the war, the Jerseys moved to Farm Street in Mayfair, and when their house took a direct hit in the

Blitz, they rented the beautiful Old Palace on Richmond Green where Virginia spent most of the war years while her husband was away with his territorial regiment. There she at last found something more meaningful than the social round when she became honorary 'mother' to a squadron of Polish airmen fighting alongside the RAF throughout the war. One of her 'boys' was the shy and handsome Florian Martini, with whom she fell finally and deeply in love. She divorced the Earl in 1947 – he had to stage another 'adultery' – married Martini and lived quietly with him in California for the rest of her long life. He and Cary Grant, she said at the end, were the only two men she had ever truly loved. As for the Maharajah of Jaipur, he took a third wife and went on to play a prominent role in Indian politics before and after independence. He kept a photograph of Virginia on his desk for the rest of his life.

After the divorce, Grandy Jersey renounced the traditional role of his forebears, handing Osterley over to the National Trust and decamping to the island of Jersey, a place with which, apart from his name, he had no connections. In January 2013, fifteen years after his death, his art collection went up for sale at Sotheby's. The press release for the sale praises his outstanding eye for quality and acknowledges Virginia Cherrill's influence on his decision to invest in the French Impressionists, a choice that went against the grain of traditional English taste at the time. The pictures that went under the hammer during the two-day sale included outstanding examples of works by Monet, Sisley, Pissarro, Gauguin, Boudin and Dufy, among others. It was, said Sotheby's, an exceptional collection assembled with discrimination and love. Grandy Jersey, who'd grown up in what he saw as the museum-like stuffiness of Osterley, put it more simply: 'I wanted pictures that were pleasant and happy to live with.'

MAIN SOURCES

Chaplin, Charlie: *My Autobiography*. Bodley Head, 1964.

Maland, Charles: *Chaplin and American Culture: The Evolution of a Star Image*. Princeton University Press, 1989.

Seymour, Miranda: *Chaplin's Girl: The Life and Loves of Virginia Cherrill*. Simon and Schuster, 2009.

12

Actors and Activists: Theatre's Golden Couple

Dame Sybil Thorndike CH DBE
(1882-1976)
Lewis (later Sir Lewis) Casson
(1875-1970)
Flat 98 1938-1976

THUMB THROUGH ANY ONE OF THE DOZENS OF books written about Sybil Thorndike and the stamina of this extraordinary woman will leave you breathless. In a theatrical career lasting sixty-five years she appeared in over three hundred plays, ranging from Greek tragedy and Shakespeare to Grand Guignol, light comedy and farce, to say nothing of film, television and radio performances and poetry recitals. Lewis Casson's life was hardly less full.

Working as actor, director, producer and theatre manager, often sharing the stage with his wife, one project flowed into the next, others always in the pipeline. The two of them appeared everywhere, from the West End to provincial reps, church halls and Welsh miners' clubs – Sybil also adding hours of high-profile political campaigning to this relentless artistic programme. The couple's energy was legendary. The actor Emlyn Williams recalled seeing them in Oxford, packing in a bustle and dashing for the London train after a one-off performance of *Medea*, one of Sybil's most acclaimed – and exhausting – roles. They sprang into a waiting taxi, Sybil calling to Lewis to remember the Thermos. 'The youngest middle-aged couple I have ever seen,' commented Williams admiringly.

Sybil had wanted to live in Swan Court ever since she'd

Sybil Thorndike and Lewis Casson with a favourite blue vase at home in flat 98, 1960s. Sybil chose the vase, a present from Lewis, as her Desert Island Discs luxury. A statuette of Sybil as St. Joan can be seen on the shelf behind.

watched it being built, thinking it just like a monastery, and flat 98 certainly had something of the monk's cell in comparison to the Cassons' previous large houses in Carlyle Square and Oakley Street. However, '98' – as it was always called – offered a refreshingly simple way of living for a couple now in their middle years with children grown and flown. Sybil found the small kitchen perfect for making breakfast and light suppers, the Swan Court restaurant convenient for lunches alone or with friends. Lewis – good with his hands – even found space in the sitting-room for china-mending. The Cassons were known throughout the block, their famous friends a talking point and Lewis sometimes to be seen, still in pyjamas and dressing gown, walking to the King's Road to fetch his newspaper. The Cassons' grandson-in-law, journalist Tom Pocock, who also followed this tradition, said that when striped flannelette and carpet slippers were no longer to be seen in the morning streets of SW3, the old Bohemian Chelsea had truly gone.

Streams of visitors, many of them household names, made their way to the sixth floor to bask in the warm Casson welcome. Sir Alec Guinness was a regular over the years, as was Laurence Olivier, a protégé of Sybil's. Olivier's son Tarquin recalled visiting with his father and being allowed to practise on the piano. John Gielgud remembered ringing the bell and hearing Sybil – an accomplished musician – singing hymns as she came to the door. Sheridan Morley, one of Sybil's biographers, documented many happy hours in the 'famous flat'. Departing guests were always accompanied to the lift, sinking downwards to Sybil's diminishing cries of 'Lewis, aren't they *darlings?*' The lift's elegant scissor gates allowed the sound to travel to the floor below before cutting out, and the comments weren't always so complimentary. The Cassons' granddaughter Diana Devlin remembered hearing her grandmother call out tartly to Lewis, 'Thank *goodness* she's stopped...' before Sybil's voice was cut off, leaving Diana in descent to the ground floor anxiously wondering what grandparental convention she'd flouted.

Sybil had first met the man she was to marry in Dublin Zoo in 1908. Lewis was wearing a shabby coat with a hat drawn down over his eyes and looked, she said, as though he would fight you if you gave him the chance. This attacking approach to life set the tone for what was often to be a stormy union. It was usually politics that got them going, Lewis' violence the more analytical and controlled, while Sybil's exploded all over the place in blazing enthusiasm for everything she encountered. Someone, possibly Noël Coward, commented that nobody loved anyone as much as Sybil loved everyone, this unflagging passion sometimes rather wearing for those around her. More endearing was her desire to see something praiseworthy in everyone, even those she disliked, once describing an acquaintance as an awful bore – but tremendously good at cooking rhubarb. Towards the end of her life, Sybil regretted that she and Lewis had been 'such violent people'. Perhaps it helped her career; she took the view that unless you were a hysterical character, you couldn't play hysterical parts.

A woman of hugely generous spirit, loved and admired by family and friends, Sybil was treated with respect by anyone who'd been on the receiving end of one of her legendarily sharp retorts. 'The stiletto', Ralph Richardson called it. 'Oh, yes, she could stab!' agreed Diana Devlin. Towards the end of her career, Sybil played the Grand Duchess in Laurence Olivier's film *The Prince and the Showgirl* with Marilyn Monroe. Sheridan Morley recounts the occasion when Monroe, a notoriously bad timekeeper, was made to apologise to Dame Sybil for keeping her waiting for an hour to start filming. 'Not at all,' said the Dame, icily gracious. 'I'm sure we're all very glad to see you… now that you are here, that is.' But disapproval soon gave way to professional generosity. At first sceptical about Monroe's playing, Sybil watched the rushes and told Olivier that Marilyn was perfect in the role. 'I was the old ham,' she commented later. 'Marilyn knew exactly what to do on the screen; I never did.'

Sybil Thorndike became one of the greatest theatrical stars of her time but, lacking conventional good looks or any marketable sexual allure, she'd had some handicaps to overcome on her way to the top. What she had in abundance was a crusading spirit, a moral force and a vibrant personality that made her magnetic on stage; these qualities never more evident than when, in her early forties, she played St. Joan. Twenty years in the profession had already brought her distinction and an honorary doctorate from Manchester University, but her playing of the charismatic, tortured Maid of Orleans took her to the very peak of her career, where she remained for most of the next decade. Actress and character were perfectly matched. 'A woman who argues about everything like blazes was bound to be attracted to a woman who ends in blazes', wrote the critic James Agate. As for Sybil, she relished Joan's warrior nature: 'I love playing a woman who has a touch of masculinity… feminine wiles I can't manage at all – and I don't want to.' Fifty years later she told Sheridan Morley that with St. Joan, she felt she'd reached something she could never reach again, and that she never really wanted to do anything else.

Bernard Shaw had been toying with the idea of a play about Joan of Arc for twenty years before it saw the light of day. Curiously, Sybil too had long fancied the character. The Cassons threw themselves into the production, starting with a visit to Shaw's home where he read the entire play to

Promotional postcard for St. Joan by Bernard Shaw, New Theatre, London, March 1923.

them, acting every part. Rehearsals began in February 1924, with Lewis co-directing with Shaw and playing the English Chaplain de Stogumber who argues for Joan's execution. The cast included Raymond Massey and Ernest Thesiger, with the fourteen-year-old Jack Hawkins as the Page.

The first night at the West End's New Theatre caused a sensation. People began queueing for seats at 5am, dozens of applications for tickets had to be refused and the curtain went up on an auditorium packed with celebrities. The public went mad for the production, packing out over five hundred performances at the New Theatre and then subsequently at the Regent Theatre in King's Cross. Reviewers – often tepid about Shaw's play – adored Sybil's Joan. The critic JD Trewin called it one of the overwhelming performances of the first half of the twentieth century. The play did well by both author and actress: in 1925 it brought Shaw the Nobel Prize for literature and in 1931, after the last West End revival, Sybil Thorndike was made a Dame.

Seven years later, when the Cassons arrived in Swan Court, they had become a nationally famous theatrical couple with a packed professional life that would have been more than enough to absorb the energies of most people. Not so Sybil and Lewis, who were no less passionate about their political commitments than they were about theatrics, such interests showing no sign of diminishing as they grew older. A search through the letters pages of the *Manchester Guardian* and *The Times* over the years throws up a flow of impassioned letters from the Swan Court address. Sybil had long used her professional skills in public speaking, her superb voice reverberating on platforms up and down the country in support of a never-ending series of theatrical, political and women's causes. She spoke at settlements in the East End of London and at Welsh miners' political rallies. She supported votes for women in the suffragette years and nuclear disarmament in her old age. She campaigned against censorship in the theatre and for refugee children in the Spanish Civil War, for conscientious objectors, striking miners, Indian independence… the list goes on and on, her passionate advocacy earning her a place on Hitler's list of people to be eliminated when Germany invaded Britain. She spoke up for the poor, the neglected and the powerless,

An active member of the Labour Party and passionate campaigner, Sybil holds a copy of the left-wing newspaper The Morning Star *with headlines about the Vietnam war. 1960s.*

and, in particular, for pacifism, which, unlike many of her contemporaries, she embraced wholeheartedly for the rest of her life.

Although Lewis shared many of her passionate enthusiasms, fiery marital slanging-matches often resulted when their opinions clashed. All their homes were hotbeds of argument, said Sybil, mealtimes often the setting for verbal attack. Younger family members recalled an occasion at the Casson family home in Wales when they escaped to the woods, leaving the adults shouting at each other round the dining table. Religion, ethics and politics were high on the list of controversial subjects. As Diana Devlin remembered, 'It was nothing to find yourself covering the nature of patriotism over the soup... democracy during the roast beef... pacifism with the jam tart and the existence of God as you sank back over your coffee.' Whatever the subject, life in '98' was never dull and often noisy. What the neighbours thought – if any of this rumpus penetrated the walls of '98' – is not known; perhaps they put it down to the natural excitability of theatrical folk. The power of Sybil's voice was unrivalled. When Peggy Ashcroft, as Desdemona to Paul Robeson's Othello, found her Willow Song drowned each night by a noisy scene change, Sybil, who was playing Emilia, told them to wait until she was speaking as she could outshout anything.

By her forties, Sybil Thorndike had achieved an unassailable position – shared with Edith Evans – as Queen of the English Stage, and, to many, a shining example of feisty womanhood. In Muriel Spark's novella, *The Prime of Miss Jean Brodie*, set in the nineteen-thirties, the redoubtable Miss Brodie, bent on turning her class of girls into the crème de la crème, instructs them on deportment: 'Form a single file now, please, and walk with your heads up, *up*, like Sybil Thorndike, a woman of noble mien.' Alongside his formidable wife, Lewis was often seen as the Svengali largely responsible for her success, ignoring the fact that, as director, producer and theatre manager, he was now among the top ten in his profession. Working continuously in the West End, he still fitted in charity galas and Sunday matinées with Sybil, and occasional trips to the provinces. Juggling artistic, commercial and popular needs, he directed everything from Shakespeare to experimental German Expressionist pieces. Opinion was divided as to whether Sybil's career was helped or hindered by working so regularly with her husband, whose directing style could be dogmatic. Stern and brusque in rehearsals, his actors were often terrified. John Casson felt that his father's violent nature, in general kept under control by willpower, showed itself in the ferocity of his attack upon his work. 'He's impossible,' Sybil would tell his actors. 'I can't think why I married him.' Asked once whether she had ever contemplated divorce, she replied, 'Divorce, never. Murder, often!'

When war broke out in 1939, the Cassons embraced the challenge with their usual fervour. On October 14th, all Chelsea turned out for a concert at the Air Raid Protection (ARP) station in Hortensia Road. 'There were lots of vulgar sketches', wrote Joan Wyndham in her diary, '...men dressed up as commandants with false bosoms, and awful jokes about what went on in the blackout.' But best of all, she thought, was the grand finale. 'Lewis Casson – last seen playing Polonius to John Gielgud's Hamlet – dashed out to a fanfare of trumpets in his blue boiler suit and hurled himself once more, dear friends, into the breach, raising the roof.'

When, in 1941, a bomb landed just behind Swan Court's North Block, the services were knocked out and '98' became temporarily uninhabitable. Unruffled by the lack of domestic comforts, the Cassons took to the road like strolling players, touring thirty-seven South Wales towns and villages in ten weeks, playing *Macbeth*, *Medea* and *Candida* in freezing village halls packed with miners and their families, most of whom had never seen a play before. The Cassons always relished this kind of stripped-down theatre, devoid of scenery or a smart audience. Lewis lived up to his Celtic roots, playing with all the emotional rhetoric of a Welsh preacher and ending each show with hymns and *Land of My Fathers*. In 1944 Sybil joined the legendary Laurence Olivier–Ralph Richardson Old Vic season at the New Theatre, playing, among many other roles, Margaret to Olivier's Richard III and Aase to Richardson's

Peer Gynt, as well as the Nurse in *Uncle Vanya* and, in 1946, Jocasta in *Oedipus Rex*.

Early in the war, the Cassons' son John, in command of a Fleet Air Arm bomber squadron, was reported missing, believed killed, in a raid over Norway. Then friends heard Lord Haw-Haw (William Joyce) boasting in a propaganda broadcast from Germany that the son of Dame Sybil Thorndike had been captured, information later confirmed by the Admiralty. One wonders if the Cassons knew that, before the war, in flat 82 – identical to theirs and directly below – the young William Joyce had been a guest and protégé of their Hitler-loving neighbour Dorothy Eckersley. (See chapter 13.)

After the war, Lewis received his knighthood for services to the theatre. They were back in '98' and life continued at full stretch. Developing new roles, reprising old ones, touring separately and together, at home and abroad, growing older but showing little sign of cutting back, they had become an institution. Critic Philip Hope-Wallace put his finger on it: 'This couple is wonderful in the sense that the Fire Brigade and the District Nursing Service is wonderful and as the Metropolitan Police used to be. They have indeed 'done the State some service'.' Full of honours, the Cassons lived on in '98' till the ends of their lives. Lewis died in 1970, and when Sybil followed him six years later, two thousand people attended a service of thanksgiving in Westminster Abbey, where her ashes were buried in the choir aisle. She was the first member of her profession since Henry Irving, and the first actress, to be so honoured.

MAIN SOURCES

Conversations with the Cassons' granddaughters, Diana Devlin and Penny Pocock, November 2016.

Casson, John: *Lewis and Sybil*. Collins, 1972.
Croall, Jonathan: *Sybil Thorndike: A Star of Life*. Haus Publishing, 2008.
Devlin, Diana: *A Speaking Part: Lewis Casson and the Theatre of his Time*. Hodder and Stoughton, 1982.
Morley, Sheridan: *Sybil Thorndike: A Life in the Theatre*. Weidenfeld and Nicolson, 1977.
Sprigge, Elizabeth: *Sybil Thorndike Casson*. Victor Gollancz, 1971.
Wyndham, Joan: *Love Lessons: A Wartime Diary*. Heineman, 1985.

13

A Risky Affair
Captain Peter Pendleton Eckersley
(1892-1963)
Mrs Frances 'Dorothy' Eckersley
(1893-1971)
Flat 82 1931-1940

IN THE SPRING OF 1907, FIFTEEN-YEAR-OLD PETER Eckersley and his best friend re-built an old chicken hut in the grounds of Bedales School in Hampshire. Wavy Lodge, as they called it, housed their homemade wireless receiver, plus a mobile transmitter that they could trundle across the school grounds to a distant cricket pitch where they relayed match scores back to the hut. Eckersley was to spend many of his schooldays in this comfortingly eccentric den, the perfect place in which to explore the delights of radio and girls, two sometimes competing obsessions that were to lead, two decades later, to a national scandal and the ruin of his brilliant career.

Eckersley had been fascinated by the idea of wireless since watching his older brother Tom experimenting in the holidays. He talked later of this first glimpse of what was to become a lifelong passion. He'd seen polished brass balls with great sparks tearing between them and beautiful ebonite instruments with needles flowing gently over a scale. 'The whole tactile feeling of those things engrossed me... I knew I must be a radio engineer. It was love at first sight,' he said.

After the outbreak of war, Eckersley left his electrical engineering course at Manchester University to join the Royal Flying Corps, testing and developing the use of wireless in aircraft target-spotting for the Royal Artillery. But there was always time for fun: posted to Cairo, he wined and dined nightly at Shepherd's Hotel, galloped the Colonel's charger across the desert at dawn, and lost his virginity to a dance-hall girl called Gaby. In 1917, back in England and promoted to Captain, he walked down the aisle of Holy Trinity Church, Sloane Street with his country-loving twenty-two-year-old bride Stella Grove.

By 1919 Eckersley was working as a wireless engineer for the Marconi Company. The timing was perfect: a passion for radio was infecting the whole country. Dame Nellie Melba's broadcast in 1920 created a sensation and sparked a demand from amateur enthusiasts for something – anything – to listen to in English. Marconi won the bid to build and run a small transmitter exclusively for amateurs and in February 1922, Eckersley was told to make it happen. He recruited a team of seven from Marconi's design department and put them to work in a long low hut in the village of Writtle in Kent, where the Eckersley family now lived. Big things can happen in small huts, he said.

The Writtle hut and what happened in it has won an indelible place in radio history, but the first broadcasts that came from it every Tuesday night were no more than a very orderly and respectable series of gramophone records, each preceded by a short announcement. Then, one Tuesday, tanked up with fish and chips and several gins in the local pub, Eckersley roared up the lane on his motorbike and took over the microphone. That night he was firing on all cylinders, a matchless combination of comedian, actor and chattering radio buff. Everything poured into the mike – songs, rhymes, pub stories, anything but records and certainly no official pauses. Radio entertainment had begun.

Eckersley's furious bosses issued an official reprimand – but then letters began arriving by the sackful, pleading for more. After that, Tuesday evenings with Eckersley behind the mike became a ritual for radio amateurs all over the country. Windows were closed, clocks stopped, a cloth thrown over the parrot cage, and it was time to put on the headphones and tune the cat's whisker to the magical spot.

By April 1922 the Marconi Company had begun a second provisional broadcasting service from London, call sign 2LO. Other regional companies followed and gradually, after many months of wrangling, the British Broadcasting Company lurched into life. On the morning of December 30th, a tall young Scot called John Reith, immaculate in bowler hat and striped trousers, arrived to take over the reins. He was autocratic, strait-laced and restlessly ambitious, and – like almost everyone else involved – he knew nothing about broadcasting. He needed a Chief Engineer and Eckersley got the job.

The first task was to build a London transmitter. Eckersley climbed to the roof of Marconi House on Kingsway, surveyed the skyline, and then set off to find the chimney of

Captain Peter Eckersley, the BBC's first Chief Engineer, 1926.

a distant electricity generating station in Marylebone. In the next six and a half years he built up and led a team of nearly four hundred people. He turned his dream of nationwide radio transmission into a reality, negotiating behind the scenes with the Post Office and developing a wide choice of programmes. He played a key role in the first international meetings on wavelength allocation and in the preparations for empire broadcasting. By 1928, four years short of his fortieth birthday, Peter Eckersley had done more than anybody else to lay the technical foundation of broadcasting in Britain. He'd also done more than most people to antagonise his boss.

It would be hard to find two personalities less suited to working in harmony; the brilliant, mercurial, anarchic Eckersley – a hard enough challenge for any manager – versus the inflexible, socially correct and moralistic Reith. Their

| *Peter Eckersley at work at Savoy Hill, 1920s.*

working relationship began on a reasonably friendly note, the two socialising occasionally with their wives, but their fundamental differences were never far below the surface. The BBC's mission may have been to inform, educate and entertain, but for Reith it was the first two that mattered. A little entertainment was all right as the icing on the cake, but only if it passed the 'maiden-aunt' test. Eckersley wanted argument, investigation and a bit of fun and controversy, and he had no time at all for the sensibilities of the nation's maiden ladies.

By 1926 broadcasting had extended over the whole country and the British Broadcasting Company, complete with Royal Charter, morphed into the British Broadcasting Corporation, its new public status confirmed by dumping the directors and appointing a board of Governors. To Reith's Chief Engineer, the prospect of a rigid public service administration stifling the artistic freedom of directors and producers was anathema. For Reith, it was the BBC's job to control – or even stamp out

– any hint of undisciplined creativity. He became more and more autocratic, and Eckersley, always on a short fuse, made things worse by firing off a series of memos criticising his boss' various committees. Then, in 1928, at the BBC in Savoy Hill, Eckersley sealed his fate when he bumped into Dorothy Clark, the estranged wife of his colleague Edward Clark, the BBC's Music Adviser. It was love at first sight.

Born in 1893 into the celebrated literary Stephen family, Dorothy was a cousin of Virginia Woolf. There were politics in her background; her mother had been a suffragette and Labour Party supporter. Dorothy grew up glamorous and headstrong and she liked life seasoned with more than a pinch of political extremism. After training at RADA, she went on the stage. By the time she was thirty she'd toured extensively in America and Britain, produced a child out of wedlock in each country, had them both adopted, married Edward Clark and given birth to their son James. The marriage foundered, and when she first set eyes on Eckersley she was separated and looking about her for the next big thing.

The badly smitten Eckersley lost his head and began a reckless affair, flaunting Dorothy openly at the BBC, dining with her in fashionable restaurants and spending nights at her flat. His wife Stella knew nothing. Then, in September 1928, he hatched a plan to take his mistress with him to Berlin, where he was to visit the headquarters of the German Broadcasting Organisation. Bizarrely, this illicit trip was conceived with Dorothy's complacent husband, who thought it would be fun for the Clarks to travel as man and wife, with Eckersley alongside. In Berlin the ménage à trois was officially welcomed by Hans Bredow, the head of German Broadcasting. Herr Bredow drove them to their hotel, taking the opportunity on the way to grope Dorothy under the car rug. Years later, Eckersley's son Myles found a photograph of the happy party during their trip, smiling into the sun, enjoying the delights of Bredow's yacht on the Wansee.

Back in London, Stella was still in the dark and everything went on as usual until, in January 1929, her husband went a step too far. In Brussels to represent the BBC at a crucial meeting about European wavelength allocation, he turned up for official receptions with Dorothy on his arm. The Senior Engineers, particularly those who had been at Writtle, knew and liked Stella and were outraged by Eckersley's behaviour. Having a mistress was one thing; flaunting her at Savoy Hill and in Brussels on BBC business was too much. They told Eckersley the affair would have to stop. Typically, he took no notice. Then, at the end of January, the story found its way to Reith.

The popular version of this still-talked-about episode in the BBC's history is that Peter Eckersley lost his brilliant career as a consequence of his boss' Calvinistic attitude to adultery. The MP Robert Boothby put about a biblical version of the story, saying, 'The prophet Reith did say unto Peter, 'My son, you have strayed from the paths of righteousness and you are dismissed''. This was a bit too simplistic. Certainly Reith had strong Christian views and, perhaps more importantly, saw the BBC as guardian of the nation's values. He was deeply disapproving but, as his diaries show, he did try to save the situation. He knew that Eckersley's pioneering technical brilliance was crucial to the BBC and that they could ill afford to lose him, but he had a crisis on his hands. His Senior Engineers were saying they wouldn't work with Eckersley and now the puritanical Governors were baying for his blood. Reith called Eckersley and Dorothy to his flat and, in a fraught meeting lasting from nine at night until three-thirty the next morning, tried to convince them that if Eckersley didn't dump his mistress, he would lose his job. None of this had any effect. In his diary, Reith wrote that both Eckersley and 'the woman' had talked 'the most appalling rot': 'They seemed quite immovable. She is thoroughly bad.' For a month the argument raged on, Eckersley saying he was going to get divorced and that his private life was nothing to do with the BBC. The Senior Engineers and the most hard-line Governors called for immediate sacking. Others, Reith included, argued for Eckersley's resignation with the possibility of re-instatement if he went back to his family.

For Reith's BBC, briefed to uphold and promote public morality, this was no minor crisis: the whole organisation was rocked to its very core by its Chief Engineer's adulterous behaviour. In desperation Reith consulted everyone he could think of, from the Archbishop of Canterbury, who recommended dismissal, to the Commissioner of the Metropolitan Police, who said no one should be allowed to stay in the BBC after being divorced, and as for having a private life, a BBC man was like a policeman – never off duty. Reith again confronted Eckersley, who broke down and briefly went back to his wife, but a chance meeting – possibly engineered by Dorothy – re-ignited the whole affair. Eckersley packed his bags and left home for good. He handed Reith his resignation, having first negotiated a rather good deal – a lump sum of £1000 in recognition of 'valuable services', and an agreement to remain as a consultant to the BBC for a year. He also picked up lucrative consultancies from Marconi and HMV.

Eckersley's departure caused shockwaves throughout the world of radio devotees. His resignation was the most important event in BBC history, said the editor of the magazine *Popular Wireless* – 'It was not only to Peter Eckersley the engineer that the BBC was beholden, but also to Peter Eckersley the restless rebel against mediocrity and dullness.'

With money coming in and their divorces finalised, Eckersley and Dorothy were free to marry and set up home together. Swan Court, just coming out of wraps, caught their eye. A fashionable modern home in bohemian Chelsea appealed to Dorothy and she set about decorating flat 82 in the latest style. James Clark, then eight years old and living with his mother and Eckersley, remembered being fascinated by the new furniture and enjoying the sight of his own reflection in an ultra-modern glass coffee table. Eckersley found the decor far more appealing than Stella's antique furniture and country linens. It was also a perfect setting for his new wife's transformation into a political hostess.

Like many people at the time, Dorothy had been throwing herself into a series of passionate political commitments. She tried everything. She ricocheted backwards and forwards across the political spectrum, an upper-class extremist; 'obsessional, but with a Chelsea accent', said Eckersley's son Myles. She flirted with Zionism before moving on to the Independent Labour Party and then via Communism towards Fascism. She joined The Link, the National Socialist League and the Carlyle Club, attending a giddy round of meetings where she met and befriended William Joyce, the future Lord Haw-Haw, standing bail for him a couple of times when he got into legal scraps.

Now flat 82 became the setting for a regular salon, with well-known radicals of all persuasions to be seen crossing the courtyard on their way to a glass of champagne and some lively political argument. Eckersley's son thought the mood revolutionary – but in a la-di-da way, remote from any working-class grassroots. Ideologically, the soirées were as deeply confused as Dorothy herself, regular visitors including Aldous Huxley – a convinced pacifist – rubbing shoulders with Percy Wyndham Lewis, who became a Fascist

Dorothy Eckersley, Swan Court's political salonnière, 1930s.

in 1931 and considered Hitler a man of peace, the socialist and sometime communist cartoonist JF Horrabin and the pacifist-turned-communist writer Raymond Postgate. In Dorothy's Communist phase, the Soviet ambassador Ivan Maisky dropped in, following up his vodka-fuelled visit with an invitation to the Embassy for a meeting of the Society for Cultural Relations with the USSR.

Eckersley was enthralled by his wife's social success, throwing himself into the cut and thrust of the weekly parties, a genial host with a bottle and a quick-fire political opinion at the ready. His politics had generally been towards the Left, his beliefs causing clashes with Reith over the BBC's ban on

Union representation. Now, like Dorothy, he began moving towards Fascism.

Widely known as a rebel and a bit of a hell-raiser since his stormy departure from the BBC, Eckersley had arrived in Swan Court in a mood of typical devil-may-care optimism. His consultancies would pay well, commercial radio beckoned, he was in great demand as a speaker on any wireless-related topic, his international reputation and contacts were second to none. But the consultancies didn't quite materialise – the BBC never used him – and new radio projects flared and died. Gradually it became obvious that funding Dorothy's high-maintenance social life as well as supporting his first family was way beyond his income. Also, old habits dying hard, he was playing away from home again. Dorothy, suspicious, moved him to a single bedroom, denied him sex and put him on a vegetarian diet. Then, in 1935, came what his son Myles afterwards referred to as 'the fateful holiday'.

In late July, Eckersley, Dorothy and James, now twelve, took a boat to Hamburg and then explored Germany, passing through beautiful medieval towns where happy flaxen-haired crowds strolled past balconies hung with Swastikas and mingled with groups of Stormtroopers in their smart brown shirts. They saw what seemed the miracle of modern Germany unfolding before their eyes in the summer sunshine. Good housing, free hospital care and holiday camps for the happy workers, sport and gymnastics for all, a modern Nirvana. James adored the Nazi uniforms and longed to join the Hitler Youth. Like many other visitors, they saw what they wanted to see, discounting rumours that were starting to circulate about the Jews. Then, in September, the three of them attended the annual week-long Nuremberg Rally.

In the nineteen-nineties, Dorothy's son James talked at length to Myles Eckersley about this holiday, describing how they were completely bowled over by the sheer glamour of the Third Reich. The huge Hollywood movies that had enthralled them in the King's Road cinema had nothing on the spectacle they saw in Nuremberg. Massed bands, banners, ten thousand men goose-stepping, ranks of Hitler Youth shouting 'Sieg Heil!' – even Busby Berkeley couldn't compete. Dorothy, her son and, to a lesser extent, her husband, were swept away.

Once back in Swan Court, cracks began appearing in the Eckersleys' marriage. Almost the only thing they still agreed on was their admiration for Hitler and the conviction that he wanted peace. Dorothy, perhaps pondering divorce, began making notes about her husband's erratic behaviour. He had been drawn into yet another business venture, but one with distinctly sinister overtones. WE (Bill) Allen, who'd known Eckersley since 1931 when they both joined Oswald Mosley's short-lived New Party, was involved with his two brothers in setting up a syndicate to develop a commercial radio station in Europe, broadcasting in English and offering advertising to British businesses. The Allens had found influential backers, including Mosley, who'd chipped in a quarter of the costs with the agreement that a proportion of the profits were to go to the British Union of Fascists (BUF). The venture, code-named Gemona, was shrouded in secrecy to hide Mosley's involvement. Absolutely hush-hush, insisted Allen, knowing that potential advertisers would be less than delighted to learn they were financing the BUF. The syndicate was offering a good salary for a technical adviser, and the cash-strapped Eckersley signed up at once, telling Dorothy they were going to be fabulously rich. She referred to it as his mad project.

Now Eckersley began a frenzied round of visits to European countries – including Germany – trying to sell the idea of the new radio station. But in the late thirties the propaganda war was developing between Britain and

Germany; he was swimming in a murky pool. In a valiant attempt to clarify his father's activities in this period, Myles Eckersley paints a picture of a man hell-bent on making money and either unknowing or uncaring about the motivations of the people he was involved with. In addition to the BUF, he had some dubious connections in Germany – and now the British intelligence services were also nosing around. The Joint Broadcasting Committee, set up by military intelligence and MI6, was certainly a player. Maybe they were keeping tabs on Eckersley – or perhaps he was working for them on the side. Who knows?

In the meantime he was having a good deal of expensive fun, collecting two mistresses along the way. In Berlin there was Jutta, the exotic Slav, and in Paris and London there was the comforting Betty – both thrown into the mix along with Dorothy, angry and miserable in Swan Court, and Stella, demanding money for her children. As the prospects for the Gemona project diminished, expenses began to run out. Living beyond his means, neglecting his tax affairs, Eckersley was headed for bankruptcy and a breakdown.

By 1939 the Eckersleys were virtually separated. Dorothy's elegant political parties in flat 82 had all but finished; she was deep into her love affair with Germany. She and James had made more visits to Berlin, where she had made many friends in high places. She met up with sisters Unity Mitford and Diana Mosley, and joined in the fun of hanging around Hitler's favourite café, hoping for a sighting.

In the glorious summer of 1939, Dorothy took James to Berlin, where he was to enrol in the Humboldt School. They stayed, as they often did, in the Hotel Continental just off Unter den Linden, and Dorothy was lunching there one day in late August when suddenly, coming towards her across the dining room, she saw two familiar faces. William Joyce and his wife Margaret were in difficulties, pursued by the British authorities for his pro-German activities. Joyce had managed to get the two of them out of England and across Belgium to Germany in the nick of time. Confident that his German contacts would smooth his path in Berlin, he'd cashed in all his sterling only to be told that no help would be forthcoming and that if the two of them stayed on after war was declared they would be interned – in separate camps. When Margaret became hysterical, Joyce suddenly remembered that the well-connected Mrs Eckersley, last seen in Chelsea, was said to be in Berlin and staying at the Continental.

Dorothy greeted the Joyces warmly and gave them lunch. Then she took them to tea with a woman friend whose husband held an influential position in the German Foreign Office. This led Joyce to Goebbel's Propaganda Ministry and a radio audition. On September 6th, just three days after war was declared, William Joyce made his first broadcast on German radio, reading the news in English. Lord Haw-Haw was born. As his biographer Mary Kenny puts it, 'Without Mrs Eckersley, William's introduction to radio work would never have occurred and he might never have metamorphosed into Lord Haw-Haw, the best known media celebrity of his time.' And, one is tempted to add, he might never have ended up on the gallows.

After war was declared, Dorothy was caught in Berlin. Strapped for cash, she found a job broadcasting in English for the Reichs-Rundfunk-Gesellschaft, the German radio organisation. There were over a dozen people, including six women, broadcasting to Britain. Dorothy announced other broadcasters, read items herself, took part in short plays and did archive and translation work. The teenage James also broadcast, even occasionally standing in for Lord Haw-Haw. This work may have solved her problems, but it rebounded on her estranged husband at home. On March 14th 1940, headlines in the press broke the news that the wife of the BBC's former Chief Engineer was broadcasting propaganda for the enemy. Her voice had been heard on the same wavelength as Lord Haw-Haw. By now, Eckersley had a substantial dossier with British Intelligence and in May, investigators broke into the Swan Court flat. Although they found nothing incriminating, they made it clear to him that although he would not be interned, as far as any serious war work was concerned, his past relationship with Dorothy had made him a pariah. Bankrupt and unemployable, when his current mistress, the writer Dorothy Carrington, told him she was going to marry someone else, Eckersley cadged a shilling for the meter off her fiancé and turned on the gas. Luckily Ms Carrington arrived in the nick of time and nursed him back to health with the help of psychiatrists. The rest of his war was spent in routine jobs to pay back the money he owed to the Inland Revenue. His life, he said later, was 'shabby'.

By 1943, Dorothy Eckersley's broadcasting career in Berlin had petered out, and she was living on a tiny wage for archive work, eked out by selling off her furs, couture clothes, and even her underwear. James' love affair with the Nazis did not survive the news of Dunkirk and other Allied setbacks, and in the Berlin hotbed of rumour and denunciations he and his mother were in a dangerous position. On Christmas Eve 1944, as the war began to turn against the Germans, they were arrested by the Gestapo and interned. James said afterwards that he owed his life to his mother; with her grand imperial manner, resourcefulness and a few still-powerful contacts, she had kept them from the concentration camps. At the end of the war they were handed over to the British Army. 'I know your sort. God help you!' said the Military Policeman who escorted them.

In October 1945, Dorothy and James were flown back to England and immediately arrested by the police before being taken to London and charged with conspiring to assist the enemy in time of war. 'I didn't know that anything I did was of such importance,' she commented naïvely. Up at the Old Bailey in December, they both pleaded guilty. Dorothy's defence counsel – somehow paid for by Eckersley – depicted her as a hopelessly opinionated amateur. Nevertheless, as a pronounced and unrepentant pro-Nazi and admirer of Hitler, she got a year in Holloway. James, being young and seen as under his mother's influence, was bound over for two years.

After her release from prison, Dorothy was still supported in part by Peter Eckersley, and they continued to meet regularly. With her political fervour diminished but ever in need of a big idea, she became an ardent Roman Catholic. She settled a few doors from the Brompton Oratory in Kensington and died in 1971. Eckersley stayed in Chelsea, first in Pont Street and then in Hasker Street, always with some female companion on his arm and living on a few hundreds a year, most of which he owed. He died in 1963, leaving just enough to settle his outstanding debts.

The full story of Eckersley's rise and fall at the BBC and the rest of his tumultuous life is told by his son Myles in his book *Prospero's Wireless*, which also goes into great detail about his father's role in the technical development of radio. It's a fascinating – and at times, painful – story of this brilliant, tricky man, whose combination of technical genius and fiery temperament caused him, and often others around him, so much anguish. Peter Eckersley climbed high and fell hard in his BBC career, but some degree of closure came two years before his death during the Corporation's fortieth birthday celebrations in 1962. The Institute of Electrical Engineers gave a party to launch the first volume of Asa Briggs' *History of*

A Risky Affair

Back in the fold, October 24th 1961. (From second left) Professor Asa Briggs, Peter Eckersley, Lord Reith and BBC Director General Hugh Carleton Greene at the launch of The Birth of Broadcasting, the first volume of Asa Briggs' History of Broadcasting in the United Kingdom.

Broadcasting in the UK, and there, photographed alongside the BBC's Director-General Hugh Carleton Greene and shoulder to shoulder with Lord Reith for the first time since 1929, was Captain Peter Eckersley. The body language between them is chilly, but the maverick midwife of British public service broadcasting does have his place at last in the history books. The Writtle hut where Eckersley began it all can be seen in the Sandford Mill Museum in Chelmsford, where each year it is the focus of International Marconi Day.

MAIN SOURCES

Briggs, Asa: *The History of Broadcasting in the United Kingdom. Volume I: The Birth of Broadcasting.* Oxford University Press, 1961.

Cullen, Stephen Michael: Strange Journey: The Life of Dorothy Eckersley in *The Historian*, Autumn 2013.

Eckersley, Miles: *Prospero's Wireless: PP Eckersley, A Biography.* Myles Books, 1997.

Griffiths, Richard: *Fellow Travellers of the Right: British Enthusiasts for Nazi Germany 1933–1939.* Oxford University Press, 1983.

Higgins, Charlotte: *This New Noise: The Extraordinary Birth and Troubled Life of the BBC.* Faber, 2015.

Kenny, Mary: Germany Calling: *A Biography of William Joyce, Lord Haw-Haw.* Max Press, 2008.

McIntyre, Ian: *The Expense of Glory: A Life of John Reith.* HarperCollins, 1993.

Murphy, Sean: *Letting the Side Down.* Sutton Publishing, 2003.

Scannell, P and Cardiff, D: *A Social History of British Broadcasting. Vol. 1, 1922–1939: Serving the Nation.* Blackwell, 1991.

Stuart, Charles (ed): *The Reith Diaries.* Collins, 1975.

14

A Controversial Historian
Arthur (later Sir Arthur) Wynne Morgan
Bryant CH CBE (1899–1985)
Sylvia Mary Bryant (1900-1950)
Flat 97 1934-1939

O<small>N THE EVENING OF</small> F<small>EBRUARY</small> 19<small>TH</small> 1979, S<small>IR</small> Arthur Bryant sat down to dinner in the Vintners' Hall to celebrate his eightieth birthday, a supreme moment for a man who had spent much of his life flattering the great and the good. He was seated between a former Prime Minister and the Archbishop of Canterbury. Further down the table was the current Prime Minister, James Callaghan, plus Field Marshals, knights of the realm and an assortment of peers and peeresses. There were many congratulatory speeches. The company applauded Bryant, the favourite historian of both Churchill and Attlee, as the grand old man of British historical writing. Yet fifteen years later, with Bryant in his grave, a well-regarded historian would condemn him in print as a Nazi sympathiser, fraudulent scholar and supreme toady.

When I began researching this piece, I knew nothing about Arthur Bryant the man. Like many of my contemporaries, in my teens I read some of his books on English history, enjoying their descriptive force, their elegant prose and their ability to make you see, hear and feel the far-off times they described. I gave no thought to the accuracy or otherwise of the research that underpinned the graceful paragraphs; it was enough to fall a little in love with some dashing seventeenth-century blade, to smell the smoke of battle and to bask in Bryant's depiction of the sunlit joys of pre-industrial England. Even his frequent lapses into a cloying sentimentality could be ignored in the immediate appeal of glamorous characters and a thundering good plot. Reading about his life decades later, it was something of a surprise to discover the raging controversy that swirled around the man and his work, both at the time of writing and well on into the millennium.

In 1931, Bryant's biography of Charles II hit the headlines, becoming a Book Society choice within a month and going through seven reprints by the following summer. By the time he moved into Swan Court, his reputation was soaring and he was earning a great deal of money. From then on, for the rest of his life, the words poured out, scarcely a year passing without a new work on the bookshelves. In the nineteen-thirties alone, he produced, among other smaller works, a biography of George V, a tribute to Stanley Baldwin, a book about King Charles' England, and, between 1933 and 1938, an acclaimed three-volume biography of Samuel Pepys that cemented his reputation as an historian. To this punishing programme of research and writing he added the direction of a huge naval pageant at Greenwich and a series of radio talks for the BBC on the 'The National Character'. In 1936 he succeeded GK Chesterton as writer of 'Our Note Book' in the *Illustrated London News*, the oldest weekly column in British journalism, a task he carried out until his death nearly fifty years later. The war years saw the publication of the first two volumes of his Napoleonic Wars trilogy, *The Years of Endurance* and *The Years of Victory*, followed by *The Age of Elegance* in 1950. Working for him in his later years, his secretary and biographer Pamela Street thought it little short of a miracle that he hadn't killed himself with overwork.

Not surprisingly, this frenzied life took its toll on Bryant's already disaffected marriage. In 1923, anxious to find a bride with money and good connections, he'd proposed to Sylvia Shakerley, the daughter of a knighted landowner, only discovering later that the family was on the verge of financial ruin and that in any case, their contacts were unlikely to be much use to an impecunious young man bent on making his way up the ladder. Complaining about his fiancée's lack of rich friends and her parents' refusal to cough up for a grand London wedding, he still went ahead with the marriage and set up home in Buckinghamshire, where his bride added insult to injury by failing to ingratiate herself with any of their titled neighbours. A workaholic and dedicated womaniser, Bryant proved a disastrous husband and by the time they moved into Swan Court, Sylvia was bored, unhappy and beginning a long descent into alcoholism. In 1936 he packed her off to South America, instructing her to find herself a lover, or at least, someone to love. Bryant told her he was regularly unfaithful to her and would continue to be so. If she wanted a divorce, he said, he could give her an address just off St. James' Square where she would find plenty of evidence of his infidelities, behaviour somewhat inconsistent with the honeyed words in support of old-fashioned values that were appearing under his byline each week in the *Illustrated London News*. Poor Sylvia – after their divorce in 1939, she went to live in a small cottage near Salisbury Plain, where her family, dismayed by the small allowance from her ex-husband, claimed she was forced to supplement her income by providing favours for the soldiers garrisoned nearby. Whether true or not, she eventually remarried, but succumbed to alcoholism a few years later.

Bryant's colourful and busy love life continued apace, disgruntled letters from dumped girlfriends still dropping onto the mat in his eightieth year. Not long after ditching Sylvia, he married Anne Brooke, niece to the white Rajah of Sarawak, who endured his insatiable womanising for ten years before they parted. At the age of eighty-one he proposed to the Dowager Duchess of Marlborough, who seems to have accepted before realising that she couldn't stay the course. Quite apart from the serial adultery, he would have been a tough proposition for any potential partner; his assistant Pamela Street, while admitting he had a certain loveableness, often found her employer bewildering, unreasonable, inconsiderate, and sometimes extremely bad-tempered.

During the thirties, Bryant became increasingly absorbed in the promotion of right-wing politics, an edgy activity that nearly proved his undoing. Always ultra-conservative, in the run-up to the war he progressed from Chamberlainite appeasement to Nazi fellow-travelling. In 1934 he had published *The Man and the Hour*, a collection of essays on world statesmen in which he praised Hitler as a mystic whose inspired leadership was creating a happy, disciplined and self-sufficient Germany well able to co-exist with differently governed neighbouring states. In January 1939, his admiration for the Führer undimmed, as general editor of the right-wing National Book Association he chose *Mein Kampf* as Book of the Month.

Bryant was acknowledged even by his close friends to be a past master at flattery, a weapon he used to great effect in his climb to the heights of social and political life, silken words and expensive dinners an important part of his armoury. By the end of the thirties he'd tucked away a great deal of money, secured his reputation as a popular historian and achieved entrée to the inner sanctums of Downing Street. Known as a useful man when it came to promoting appeasement, in the summer of 1939 he attended a secret meeting in Germany with Hitler's adjutant Walther Hewel in an attempt to convince the Nazi government of the inevitable consequences of attacking Poland. This doomed mission was kept under wraps. The visit had been approved 'entirely unofficially' by Number Ten, Chamberlain offering to pay Bryant's expenses from Secret Service funds.

Apologists for Bryant are quick to point out that he was far from alone in his naïve support for Fascism and the Nazi regime during the thirties. Swan Court had its share of those in sympathy with him. The majority began to lose faith by 1939 as the reality of events pressed home. Not so Bryant: buoyed up by huge book sales, the ear of people in high places, and unlimited opportunities for expressing his ideas in the press, he felt invincible. In an act of supreme self-confidence, in the first months after war was declared he sent the manuscript of his latest book, *Unfinished Victory*, to his publishers, Macmillan. The editor who read it told Harold Macmillan that it could not be published as it condoned Nazism. Macmillan took the view that they were publishers, not policemen, and went ahead, his feelings about the book wavering back and forth until, some time after it came out, he resolved never to publish Bryant again.

Unfinished Victory appeared in the bookstores at the beginning of 1940, during the last months of the 'Phoney

War'. Its strongly anti-Semitic text was, says historian Andrew Roberts, as complete an apologia for Nazism as it is possible to imagine being published at such a time. Bryant's thesis boiled down to broad support for the new Germany under Hitler's inspired leadership, backed up by a raft of examples aimed at proving that Nazi policy towards the Jews was the consequence of their unreasonable dominance in many areas of German life. Inflammatory stuff, one would think, but the book found favour with many reviewers and readers and Bryant was at first steadfast in his support for it, sending complimentary copies to the royal family and to friends in high places. Then, as the 'Phoney War' came to an end in May 1940, things got serious. Churchill, the anti-appeaser, had replaced Chamberlain as Prime Minister, and many prominent Nazi sympathisers were rounded up and interned. Doubts were raised in some high places about Bryant's allegiance, up to and including the suggestion that he too should face internment. This was rejected, one reason being that those in charge recognised that his skills could be put to good use. Oxford historian Hugh Trevor-Roper – then working in Intelligence at Bletchley Park – later recalled the official view that Bryant could be 'turned' as a propagandist in support of the war effort. This reaction from some of those he was desperate to impress appears to have hit home; Bryant ran for cover, saying he was 'in disgrace', and went on a buying spree in an attempt to remove as many copies of *Unfinished Victory* as possible from the bookshops. Then, switching overnight from sustained hostility to Churchill to a slavering devotion, he churned out a popular history of England from 1340 to 1940. *English Saga*, published at the end of 1940, may have been short on academic rigour but it was certainly high on patriotism. It placed the country's plight firmly in an historical context, England seen as 'fighting a war of redemption, not only for Europe, but for her own soul', a patriotic approach that hit a chord in the national psyche and shot the book to the top of the bestseller lists. It sold in its thousands, raising morale, winning praises from Churchill and setting Arthur Bryant firmly back on his pedestal as the nation's favourite guardian of the national story. His friend and sometime critic, the historian AL Rowse, said that in his efforts to make it up with Churchill, Bryant was playing all the old records about how wonderful the English people were.

But it worked, and after that, Bryant could do no wrong. Book after book poured out of him, lacking the depth of

| Arthur Bryant, back in favour and heading for a knighthood in 1955.

scholarship he'd achieved before the war but all singing more or less the same song. His brand of late-Victorian patriotism had been immensely successful in the past and he saw no reason to alter it. Dismissed by academics, his public still adored him and feasted on everything he produced. The honours came from both sides of the House – a knighthood from Churchill, followed in 1967 by the coveted Companion of Honour from Harold Wilson. But as the sixties moved into the seventies, a new breed of popular historian began to overtake him and he turned increasingly to journalism to promote his championship of reactionary causes, from admiration for Enoch Powell to detestation of the Common Market, writing his regular punchy articles for the *Illustrated London News* and joining Beaverbrook's stable of journalists at the *Sunday Express*. Nevertheless, old admirers of his books kept the faith. 'Oh my', wrote Lord Reith, 'how magnificently you are to be envied in what you have done and in what you will leave behind'. 'I have devoured everything you have ever written', wrote PG Wodehouse from his Long Island exile. Harold Wilson had every one of Bryant's books in the Chequers library, telling journalists he admired *English Saga* above all works in the English language. Given Bryant's continuing status within the establishment, it's unsurprising that in 1968 a fifty-year closure rule was put on papers relating to his political activities in the thirties.

While he was in Swan Court, Bryant acquired several other properties, including rooms in Albany – useful, no doubt, for writing or shady assignations – alongside his country home in Buckinghamshire, moving between them and making it hard to pin down details of his daily life. He and Sylvia are listed on the electoral role at Swan Court for four years, during which his galloping literary success and political views would have been well known to his neighbours. No doubt opinions varied.

Meeting him in the courtyard, Dorothy Eckersley might well have asked him up for a drink, while Dame Sybil Thorndike, staunch Socialist, would have felt more like giving him a piece of her mind.

By the end of the thirties, Bryant moved from Swan Court to a substantial house at 18 Rutland Gate, where over the years he entertained his diminishing band of influential admirers to evenings where the food, the Burgundy, the candlelight and the stately Victorian setting recreated a vanished world. 'I enjoyed every minute of it', wrote John Betjeman, in thanks for one such sumptuous occasion. Life in Rutland Gate and in Bryant's final home in Salisbury's Cathedral Close perfectly reflected the man and his unabashed late-Victorian attitudes, both consolation and sadness in this love affair with the society into which he had been born, long after it had been irrevocably swept away.

When the files were opened in 1990, five years after Bryant's death, the historians got going. Andrew Roberts' *Eminent Churchillians*, published in 1994, includes a long essay branding Bryant as a Nazi sympathiser, dodgy scholar and first-class humbug. Dr Julia Stapleton jumped into the fray in an attempt to rescue Bryant's scholarly reputation, while others have insisted that his political sympathies should be recognised as typical of his age and class at the time. In 2014, W Sydney Robinson examined the man and his work in *The Last Victorians*, painting a picture of Bryant as a brilliant historian and writer whose significant early work was overshadowed by an ill-judged and inferior output in later years. As for his political beliefs and activities, said Robinson, he was naïve and misguided but certainly no traitor, and a re-evaluation of his life and work was overdue.

Academics continue to be appalled, admiring or just plain fascinated by this chameleon writer who has come to embody the nation's psychological confusion as it teetered on the brink of armed conflict. In *What Did You Do During the War?*, a 2017 study of the last throes of the British pro-Nazi Right, Richard Griffiths has used an analysis of the favourable responses to *Unfinished Victory* in 1940 to shoot down the myth that the British public was unanimously against Nazi Germany during the 'Phoney War'.

That Bryant, in his day, could write with consummate skill is not in dispute, neither is his capacity for florid over-egging of the historical cake. But, as even some of his critics have allowed, by making history a 'good read', by writing as if he were a bystander to the events he described, he brought the past to life and did encourage many who would not otherwise have done so to take a real interest in historical events. As for Sir Arthur Bryant the man, how should he be judged? Hospitable host and charmer, or smarmy flatterer with dodgy affiliations and an eye to the main chance? As with his work and his politics, no doubt there is still more to be said on both sides.

MAIN SOURCES

Obituary in *The Times*, January 24th 1985.
Cannadine, David: Review of *The Search for Justice*. In *The Observer*, August 19th 1990.
Griffiths, Richard: *What Did You Do During the War?: The Last Throes of the British pro-Nazi Right*. Routledge, 2017.
Griffiths, Richard: Essay in *The Oxford Dictionary of National Biography*, September 23rd 2004.

Kenyon, J: *The Observer*, February 18th 1979.
Northcote Parkinson, C: *A Law Unto Themselves*. John Murray, 1966.
Roberts, Andrew: *Eminent Churchillians*. Weidenfeld and Nicolson, 1994.
Robinson, W Sydney: *The Last Victorians*. The Robson Press, 2014.
Stapleton, Dr Julia: essay in Copsey, Nigel and Olechnowicz, Andrzej (eds): *Varieties of Anti-Fascism: Britain in the Inter-War Period*. Palgrave Macmillan, 2010.
Street, Pamela: *Arthur Bryant: Portrait of a Historian*. Collins, 1979.

15

The Mitford Boy
The Hon. Thomas David Freeman-Mitford (1909-1945)
Flat 19 1933-1939

―∞―

IN THE LITTLE STONE CHURCH IN THE VILLAGE OF Swinbrook in Oxfordshire there's a wall tablet erected in memory of Major Thomas David Freeman-Mitford, killed fighting in Burma in 1944, aged thirty-six. He was, says the dedication, 'a very perfect son and brother'.

In the river of words written about the notorious Mitford family in print and online, Tom, the only boy, drifts serenely along in the margins, surfacing from time to time in a brief reference or footnote as observer – and sometimes protector – of one or other of his sisters in the fall-out from their often scandalous antics. Handsome, clever, musically gifted – he was a fine pianist – Tom's position as his parents' favourite largely protected him against the worst excesses of Lord and Lady Redesdale's chaotic approach to child-rearing in a household ruled by extremism and prejudice. His mother Sydney, vague and eccentric, would almost certainly have preferred six boys and one girl, rather than the female-dominated mix she got. His sisters felt their brother always got the best of things. The family's various homes rang with the girls' cries of protest at what they saw as Tom's unreasonable advantages, wails of 'It's unfair' always countered by their parents with 'Tom's a boy. It's different for him'. This preference – the norm at the time in families like theirs – never ceased to grate with the girls, but their brother's happy, confident personality was endearing and his sisters loved and envied him in equal measure.

With classic good looks appealing to both men and women, Tom enjoyed a varied sentimental life, kicking off at Eton by attracting the attentions of James Lees-Milne. Later on, the famously bisexual Lytton Strachey also fell prey to his charm. He was involved with various beautiful women, including the startlingly chic Princess de Faucigny Lucinge and the Austrian dancer Tilly Losch, both before and during her brief marriage to the millionaire surrealist art patron Edward James. This affair did not go down too well with the Mitford family, Lord and Lady Redesdale telling James they were delighted he'd married Tilly as they'd been afraid Tom might.

A passion for all things German – the culture, the language, the philosophy and, in particular, the music – dominated Tom's life. His sister Diana remembered him spending hours at the piano when they were growing up, filling the house with Bach, Haydn, Beethoven and Mozart. At Eton, where he played the flute in the school orchestra, he was allowed a piano in his room and won the Music Prize in 1926. After Eton and Oxford he toyed with the idea of becoming a professional musician, but opted to read for the Bar. Like most of his family, Tom had Fascist inclinations and became entranced by the Nazi regime. In 1932 he was studying law in Berlin, and when Diana and Bryan Guinness went to visit, they found him intoxicated by the latest developments in German politics. 'If I were a German, I suppose I would be a Nazi,' he told Diana, sparking her first interest in Hitler.

Tom's years in Swan Court were punctuated by visits to Germany for the annual Nuremberg Rallies. Nearer home, he was vocal in support for his new brother-in-law Oswald Mosley's British Union of Fascists, joining the 20,000-strong crowd at Mosley's Earl's Court rally in July 1939. That same year, believing war was inevitable, Tom joined a territorial regiment, the Queen's Westminster's. This patriotic action may have encouraged the authorities to take a more lenient

Tom Mitford (far left) with (from left) his cousins Winston, Clementine, Diana and Randolph Churchill, and Charlie Chaplin (far right), at the Churchill home in Chartwell, Kent, in 1931.

view of his open admiration for the Nazi cause when, in 1940, his sister Diana and Mosley were imprisoned for their Fascist activities and support for Hitler. Tom – no less a follower but perhaps more circumspect in behaviour – must have taken a dim view of his eldest sister Nancy's hand in the imprisonment: she had actively campaigned for Diana to be detained, writing to Gladwyn Jebb at the Foreign Office about the dangers of her sister's pro-German inclinations. By 1943, Tom had become deeply concerned about Diana's health in prison and persuaded their cousin Winston Churchill that the Mosleys should be allowed to live together in detention. They were moved to a small house in the grounds of Holloway for the rest of the war.

A year later, fearing his regiment might be sent to fight on the soil of his beloved Germany, Tom applied to be sent to the Far East, becoming second-in-command of his battalion in Burma after turning down a staff job. He was wounded at the beginning of March 1945, and a month later his family learnt he had died.

The irascible Lord Redesdale never recovered from the loss of his beloved only son, losing all interest in everything that was to have been Tom's inheritance. He and his wife Sydney lived separately, he a virtual recluse in a cottage on their land in Northumberland, she raising goats on their remote Scottish island Inch Kenneth. She shared her home with her daughter Unity, who was confused and incontinent following her botched attempt to shoot herself in the head when Hitler declared war on Britain in 1939.

Of all the Mitford sisters, Diana had been the closest to Tom. They were more like twins than brother and sister, she wrote later. 'A day never passes when I do not think of him and mourn my loss. He was clever, wise and beautiful, he loved women and music and his family.'

MAIN SOURCES

de Courcy, Anne: *Diana Mosley*. Chatto & Windus, 2003. The whole extraordinary Mitford family is vividly re-created in a text sprinkled with little glimpses of Tom Mitford's life alongside his more notorious sisters.

Mosley, Diana: *A Life*. Faber, 1999.

16

The Passionate Bibliophile
John Davy Hayward (1905-1965)
Flat 115 1938-1939

John Hayward, editor and anthologist, always described himself as a 'man of letters'. Books were in his blood. He came from a family of writers and as a boy he spent hours playing at a make-believe desk in the attic of his parents' house, surrounded with pens, pencils and inks. His first brush with literary celebrity came early: one day on Wimbledon Common the ageing poet Algernon Swinburne paused on his daily walk to the pub to kiss the tiny Hayward in his pram. Years later, four volumes of Swinburne's poetry – bound in blue Morocco leather and costing all his pocket money – were Hayward's prized possession when he

| *John Hayward by Anthony Devas. Ink, crayon and wash. 1950.*

arrived for his first term at Gresham's School. They were, he said, his passport to maturity.

Boundlessly confident and ambitious, at eighteen years old Hayward decided it was time to break into the London literary scene. In the summer of 1923 he dropped in to the offices of the Nonesuch Press in Soho's Gerrard Street, introduced himself to the owners, David (Bunny) Garnett and Francis Meynell, and talked them into commissioning him as editor of the works of his hero, the rakish seventeenth-century poet John Wilmot, 2nd Earl of Rochester. It was an astonishing coup for Hayward and a brave move for Meynell and Garnett. To commission a totally inexperienced teenager was a leap of faith, and to publish Rochester's raunchy near-pornographic output – banned for over a hundred years – could mean prosecution. But Meynell, always an enthusiastic supporter of new talent, chose Hayward over another more established contender. Years later, on Meynell's seventieth birthday, Hayward sent him a drawing of a hand, a foot and a ladder. The inscription read 'Francis Meynell placing John Hayward's foot on the first rung of the literary ladder, 1923.'

We get a rather entrancing picture of John Hayward at this time from his prospective publishers. Meynell remembered him bright-eyed and full of gaiety, given to doing comic imitations of people and puffing trains. Garnett relished his witty anecdotes that shot out like jets of water expelled from pipes. What neither could have failed to notice were the first disabling signs of the muscular dystrophy, diagnosed in his teens, that would all too soon put him in a wheelchair for the rest of his life.

Up at Cambridge, Hayward eased himself into literary society, falling under the spell of Roger Fry, Maynard Keynes, Lytton Strachey and other leading 'Bloomsberries'. Later he was to become a stringent critic of Bloomsbury and what it stood for, but in the Cambridge of the early nineteen-twenties it represented to the young Hayward all that was intellectually exciting. Another new friend was George 'Dadie' Rylands, scholar, actor and theatre director, with whom Hayward could indulge his own acting talents. They appeared together in the Marlowe Dramatic Society's famous production of *The Duchess of Malfi*, Rylands describing Hayward's performance as the Fourth Madman as having all the zest of an inebriated gorilla. Through Rylands, Hayward got to know the hugely rich Victor Rothschild, a talented research chemist with an extravagant playboy lifestyle who shared Hayward's passion for book collecting.

It would have been impossible to ignore John Hayward in the streets of Cambridge as he rocketed around in his baby Austin or imperilled the lives of pedestrians with his wheelchair. Odd-looking, with a large, drooping bright-red

John Hayward, with appropriately erotic statue, photographed by Lee Miller in the grounds of her home at Farleys House in Sussex, 1955.

lower lip, he played up to it with flamboyant clothes set off with wide-brimmed hats and huge brightly coloured bow ties. One fellow student, later a good friend, thought him on first meeting an exhibitionist nightmare. By the time he was nineteen he'd earned a reputation among his fellow students for brilliance and erudition as well as eccentricity, his status as a commissioned editor with a possible prosecution for obscenity in the offing only enhancing his aura of stardom.

However, when *The Collected Works of John Wilmot Earl of Rochester* eventually saw the light of day in 1926, it was all a bit of a let-down. The critics didn't know how to take Rochester, said Francis Meynell, and had nothing to say about his editor's work. Hayward's father thought the book sickening and took his copy up to the attic – perhaps the same one where his little son had played at being a writer – and locked it into a trunk, away from the prying eyes of passing maiden aunts or the servants. So much, said Hayward, for the work that was going to make his reputation. The rejigging of Rochester's status from beyond-the-pale pornographer to serious poet was slow in coming; it took Graham Greene forty years before he could get his biography *Lord Rochester's Monkey* accepted by a publisher. Today, Rochester – who died at just 33 – is seen as the most considerable poet of the Restoration period, and Hayward's mature and far-sighted work helped kickstart this transformation, an extraordinary achievement for a twenty-one-year-old undergraduate.

Alongside Rochester, Hayward was also in thrall to a thoroughly contemporary voice. In 1915, T.S. Eliot published his poem *The Lovesong of J. Alfred Prufrock*. Older and more traditional readers and critics of the time thought *Prufrock* – and *The Wasteland*, which followed it seven years later – at best incomprehensible and at worst rubbish. To Hayward and his generation, the poems encapsulated the spirit of the age and all the excitements of Modernism. In 1926 Hayward met his hero. Eliot, sixteen years his senior, became his closest companion for three decades until the friendship hit the rocks on Eliot's second marriage.

By March 1933 Hayward had moved to a flat at 22 Bina Gardens in South Kensington. He painted his sitting room, filled his bookshelves, moved his desk into the bay window overlooking the garden and settled down to work and to indulging his other great love – entertaining. He adored his 'evenings', occasions when London's literary world trekked to his door, journalists, scholars and critics rubbing shoulders with anyone else who'd caught his fancy. You might meet some poets, perhaps Stephen Spender and WH Auden, alongside the Marx brothers, or James Thurber, John Betjeman and Anthony Powell chatting away to harmonica player Larry Adler, or talking films with critic Dilys Powell. It was all leavened with a pinch of aristocratic Bloomsbury, often in the person of Hayward's particular friend Lady Ottoline Morell.

Sunday evenings at Bina Gardens were more select men-only occasions centred on a nucleus of Hayward's three special cronies – T.S. Eliot, Geoffrey Faber, chairman of Faber and Faber, and Frank Morley, one of the company's founder directors. Others were drawn in from time to time and the evenings followed a regular pattern – literary gossip and lots of drink round the fire, plus practical jokes, laughter and a song or two. The poems and parodies of the evenings were even enshrined in a privately printed publication entitled *Noctes Binanianae*, a joke harking back to a regular feature of the Victorian *Blackwood's Magazine*. The founding four gave each other nicknames, Hayward dubbed Tarantula to exemplify the web he spun about them all.

Reading about Hayward's social life makes one wonder how he had any time or inclination for work, but this extraordinarily prolific critic and editor never stopped churning out the words. Always short of money, journalism provided him with a good source of income as a contributor to *The Times* and *The Times Literary Supplement*, the *New Statesman*, the *Daily Mirror*, *The Spectator* and *The Observer*, among many others. His records show an impressive output: in two years he wrote more than three hundred reviews, poking about in other writers' efforts, digging out textual mistakes and solecisms and exposing them ruthlessly to his sharp wit and scholarly criticism. One editor must have been devastated to read that her painstaking conclusions were dismissed as 'the slender progeny of mice engendered by such a mountain of research'. Such devastating attacks could imperil personal relationships: a shattering blast aimed at one of the Nonesuch editors lost Hayward the friendship of the Press's David Garnett, one of the two people to whom he owed his first big break. Small wonder that Hayward, who could be the funniest and most affectionate of companions, was also known for his peppery wit and malicious tongue, making enemies as easily as he made friends.

As the special Sunday evenings became established, Hayward's friendship with Eliot began to mature into the defining relationship of his middle years. Both men were struggling with difficulties in their romantic lives, Eliot's wife Vivienne increasingly prey to bouts of hysteria and Hayward in recovery after the ending of his relationship with Elaine Finlay, the longest lasting of his various sexual entanglements. Hayward and Eliot both enjoyed crosswords, pedantry, parody and practical jokes, with Eliot spending hours in his favourite joke shop near the British Museum. They shared a scatological sense of humour, laughing themselves silly at schoolboy howlers, Eliot dropping the formal strait-laced façade he often presented to the world. A shared home was mooted, but

Eliot was unsure. Currently lodging in a rather monastic set-up with the eccentric priest of the Anglo-Catholic church he attended in Kensington, he felt that in Bina Gardens he might be less protected from Vivienne's wayward behaviour as she edged nearer to mental breakdown.

So Hayward's life through the thirties went on in a welter of work – anthologies of Jonathan Swift and John Donne as well as journalism – and an unending round of lunches and dinners and country house weekends. There were visits to collectors anxious to pick his brains about additions to their libraries. There was the Garrick Club, where friends from the book world met once a month in an informal dining club called the 'Biblioboys'. All this activity was undertaken by an increasingly disabled man who bore his difficulties lightly. 'No saint,' said his old friend Graham Greene, 'but the bravest man I know.' Cabbies heaved his wheelchair into their taxis under instruction – 'Just tip me back headfirst, driver, don't be alarmed' – before taking him all over London. Publisher Rupert Hart-Davis remembered the challenge of heaving the chair and its heavy occupant up the steps to the Garrick before their lunches and manoeuvring it down awkward staircases in private homes. Doormen at flats all over London became accustomed to pulling Hayward up and into their foyers.

Then in September 1938 came the Munich crisis, triggering a domestic upheaval for Hayward when his Bina Gardens landlady told him that if war came, she would no longer be able to feed or look after him. Swan Court seemed a good place to move to: Eliot knew it well, and Hayward's friend Bryan Guinness would be a neighbour. On a mild sunny day in November a taxi driver deposited his curious burden in the courtyard and the porters helped the new resident into the South Block's service lift before whisking him up to his new quarters.

Flat 115 must have seemed a strange environment after the red-brick Edwardian cosiness of Bina Gardens with its large bow window and green outlook. Hayward's new home was a cool white modern box, divorced from street life, seven floors up with panoramic views over London to the east and north. As the news worsened and the threat of war became ever more real, the mild weather gave way to an icy December. The sitting room windows were lashed by freezing north-easterly winds, with a white Christmas to follow. Depression set in with news of old friends planning to leave the country; when WH Auden – known since prep school – left for America with Christopher Isherwood in January, it seemed to Hayward as though the old world was indeed dying. He took to placing his chair by the sitting room window, gloomily gazing eastwards to where he would see the German bombers when they decided to come. But the months running up to the declaration of war on September 3rd 1939 were filled with a final round of parties, neighbours popping in and out, and the companionable Sunday evenings with Eliot and others continuing. By the autumn, with the very real threat of war from the air, friends were querying the wisdom of a seventh-floor flat for someone in a wheelchair, and when Victor Rothschild offered a refuge in his house in Cambridge, Hayward reluctantly gathered up his books and papers, including his collection of Eliot's letters and draft manuscripts, and joined the exodus from the city.

Life in Merton Hall in the grounds of St. John's College was a rude shock. Safety from bombs there may have been – the Hall had an underground air raid shelter where family and guests were attended by a steel-helmeted butler – but nothing could compensate for the loss of London's literary scene. Gone were the parties, the theatre visits, the endless gossip and chat, the jolly evenings round the fire. Hayward paid for his lodgings by looking after the house and garden and cataloguing the impressive Rothschild library, keeping busy but still homesick for what he called 'his old rut' in Chelsea. When wrongly informed that Swan Court had been badly damaged in a raid, he assumed his flat had gone and wrote to Eliot about the total loss of that small corner of the 'warren' where the two of them had spent so many happy Sunday evenings.

Much of Hayward's time in the war years had been taken up with the editing of Eliot's poetry in draft, and in 1946, coming back to Chelsea, the two at last set up home together in Carlyle Mansions, a red-brick mansion block in Cheyne Walk. Hayward settled comfortably into the largest room, which he filled with books. The window faced the river and overlooked a small public garden, enabling him to make a daily study of the legs of pretty young secretaries lunching on the bench opposite. By contrast, Eliot took a small back bedroom, monastically furnished with a single bed and lit by an unshaded forty-watt light bulb. The literary world again beat a path to Hayward's door, his visitors occasionally glimpsing the shadowy figure of the great poet making his way down the dark corridor to his monkish cell. Everyone wanted to know Hayward; no literary party of any consequence was complete without him, said Lady Violet Bonham Carter.

Hayward and Eliot lasted eleven years as flatmates in Carlyle Mansions, much of their time spent working together, Hayward a critical friend in the development of Eliot's poems and plays. They became one of the sights of Chelsea as they took the air, Eliot in dark hat and formal suit pushing the wheelchair. Hayward's understanding and sympathy saw the guilt-racked Eliot through the trauma of Vivienne's death in a mental hospital in 1947, helping him to avoid a breakdown. The friendship came to a sudden end on a dark January day in 1957 when, at 6.30 in the morning, Thomas Stearns Eliot walked down the aisle of St. Barnabas Church, Kensington, with a new bride, his secretary Valerie Fletcher. He was 68, she was 30. Eliot's solicitor was best man and the only guests were Valerie's parents. The newly-weds left immediately for the south of France.

Eliot had told none of his friends about his marriage plans, merely informing Hayward by letter just before the day. It transpired that for some time he'd been stealthily removing his clothes and other belongings from the flat. Several versions of the episode swirled around their circle for years. Eliot had honoured all financial obligations to their shared life, but many of Hayward's friends felt he had been scurvily treated. The press latched on to the story and Hayward himself subsequently enjoyed fuelling the gossip, sniping at Valerie's social origins and even subtly re-awakening the hints of homosexuality and cruelty to his first wife that had dogged Eliot in the past. After some awkward attempts to remain in contact, things eventually degenerated into the sending of polite Christmas cards. It was a sad end to a deep personal attachment and a working relationship in which, over the years, Hayward's masterly editorial criticism and advice had played an important role in the fine-tuning of Eliot's genius.

Hayward continued alone in Carlyle Mansions. The little back bedroom lay dark and empty, perhaps prompting thoughts of the baffling contrast between its sparse furnishings and the previous occupant's new home in Kensington Court Mansions among Valerie's flowered cretonnes and Maples furniture. Increasingly disabled and dependent on paid help, Hayward struggled on for his remaining years, eventually becoming housebound, carried night and morning from bed to chair and back. He continued to work, publishing his final anthology, *The Oxford Book of Nineteenth Century English Verse*, in 1964. For the last twelve years of his life he edited *The Book Collector*, an idiosyncratic and scholarly publication read and loved by collectors, dealers and librarians throughout the English-speaking world. He still entertained frenetically, his home becoming a place of pilgrimage for any critic, scholar or bibliophile passing through London.

When Eliot died in January 1965, Hayward learned of it on the radio. Carlyle Mansions was besieged by the press, clamouring for a fiery reaction from an abandoned friend. But when the Poet Laureate, Cecil Day-Lewis, asked him to contribute to Eliot's obituary in *The Times*, Hayward summed up his past friend with affection. This was a generous gesture to a man who, just two years before, had inflicted a deep wound when he published his *Collected Poems* minus the original preface acknowledging Hayward's editorial contribution to the *Four Quartets*.

Hayward's last years were saddened by the rift with Eliot and blighted by increasing physical decline, which eventually left him unable even to hold a pen. And he lived to witness the slow death of the pre-war literary world of which he had been such an important part: independent publishers were disappearing and many of the great private book collections he had helped to develop were being broken up and sold, often to foreign buyers.

Hayward died in his bed on September 17th 1965. He was, said *The Times* the next day, outstanding in his generation among connoisseurs of good writing and good book production. His friend, the poet Kathleen Raine, felt his going marked the end of an era. He described himself as a 'man of letters', she said, a thing that with his death had almost ceased to exist. Hayward bequeathed his entire collection of Eliot's manuscripts to King's College Cambridge.

And what is best remembered of Hayward's work, over half a century later? For many ordinary readers it will be his 1956 *Penguin Book of English Verse*, which became the best-selling anthology of its time, knocking Quiller-Couch's *Oxford Book of English Verse* onto a back shelf and triggering twenty-six reprints in its first thirty years. Hayward chose one hundred and fifty poets writing in English over the four centuries that divided the first Elizabethan age from the second, and for five decades his choices captivated readers of all ages, defining their ideas of what English poetry was. Hayward's friend Edith Sitwell told him he had an extraordinary gift for making poems shine at their finest. This entrancing little book can be picked up second-hand today for less than a pound. It perfectly reflects the quote from John Dryden with which Hayward begins his introduction: 'The chief, if not the only, end of poetry is to delight.'

MAIN SOURCES

Obituary in *The Times*, September 18th 1965.
Gardner, Helen: *The Composition of Four Quartets*. Faber, 1978.
Gordon, Lyndall: *T.S. Eliot: An Imperfect Life*. WW Norton, 2000.
Kojecký, Roger: Essay on John Hayward in *The Oxford Dictionary of National Biography*, September 23rd 2004.
Smart, John: *Tarantula's Web: John Hayward, TS Eliot and Their Circle*. Michael Russell Ltd, 2013. The definitive book on John Hayward's life.

17
On the Wilder Shores
Lesley Blanch MBE (1904-2007)
Flat 69 1940-1944

LESLEY BLANCH WAS BARELY FIVE YEARS OLD when the man she was always to call the Traveller insinuated himself into her imagination and her heart. An exotic personage of supposedly Tartar origins, in the years before the First World War the Traveller's random visits to her Chiswick home included hours spent in her nursery, entrancing the little golden-haired girl with his magical tales of old Russia. Each visit brought an exotic gift, perhaps a dagger from the Caucasus, a samovar, an icon, a perfect Fabergé egg. As Lesley grew older, she filled the nursery with her own finds, her bookshelves packed with travellers' tales of the exotic East and the works of great Russian writers, her favourites Gogol, Pushkin and Chekhov. She begged the Traveller for stories of bygone days in Moscow or the Caucasus and at night she dreamed of rattling across Russia's snowy wastes on the Trans-Siberian Express, bound for the jewelled delights of Samarkand and stations east. Lesley Blanch was marked for life by the Traveller and his background, twin passions that went on to influence all her choices, from the clothes she wore to the homes she created, the subjects she wrote about, and the men she loved.

Lesley's initiation into the delights of sex also came courtesy of the mysterious Traveller. Possibly a previous lover of her mother and certainly a long-time friend of her parents, this dangerously alluring man was given permission to take their pretty seventeen-year-old daughter to Paris for her Easter holidays. The trip gained some spurious respectability by the presence of Lesley's French teacher, an easily-deceived chaperone much occupied with religious observances. Thus a happy de-flowering took place on the night train to Dijon, the start of an affair during which Lesley learnt a lot of things about sex, love and Russia, all of which stood her in good stead after the Traveller, in the blinking of an eye, vanished from her life. In later years and far-flung parts, she sometimes thought she caught sight of him; his curious Tartar face, the smell of his cigar, the whisk of his coat-tails through a doorway. Once she came across someone who had vague news of him, but nothing came of it. It was said he was a spy; perhaps so, but for whom was a mystery.

Lesley's adult life kicked off with a spell at the Slade School of Art, and for some years she tried her hand at illustration and theatre design. Despite a distinct talent, she found it hard to earn a living, but her way with words soon won her an entry into journalism. Always fascinated by clothes and fashion, she adored the exotic and colourful. Not for her the muted palette imposed on fashionable women of the day by Coco Chanel and her peers. In June 1935, in a passionate article she entitled 'Anti-Beige', readers of *Harper's Bazaar* were exhorted to stop playing safe and go for all things scarlet. The glossy magazine world was impressed and the next year, without any professional journalistic experience, she found herself features editor of *British Vogue*, where they gave her a secretary and nursed her along as she learnt the ropes. She never learnt to type, filing copy and writing books in longhand all her life. None of this mattered, because what she wrote was startlingly fresh and original. Audrey Withers, *Vogue's* editor for twenty years from 1941, thought her the most completely individual character you could meet in a lifetime, a free spirit, uninfluenced by anybody, let alone by anybody's opinions. She flourished at *Vogue*, writing about theatre, films, ballets and books, any off-beat topics that took her fancy and, as often as possible, about Russia and Russians. She found her writing voice, her prose vivid, her reviews sometimes savage and her opinions often challenging the gracious living ideals of the archetypal Vogue reader. What Lesley enjoyed, said her biographer, was tossing bombs into this pool of complacency. She became a personality and a treasured guest, as at home in high society, the demi-monde or bohemia as in the often run-down lodgings of her many Russian émigré friends.

The Lesley Blanch who arrived in Swan Court in the early years of the war was in her mid-thirties, between husbands, a renowned journalist, witty, opinionated and irresistibly charming. Her friend and *Vogue* colleague Anne Scott-James – no slouch when it came to brains and beauty – said Lesley made her feel like a plodding pedestrian alongside one who went through life on wings. Lesley's pink-and-white looks added to this effect; a baroque angel, said Anne, with her oval face framed in a halo of golden curls. 'I was very pretty, I will say that', Lesley wrote later. 'I always had a swarm of

'A baroque angel with golden curls.' Lesley Blanch, photographed at home by Norman Parkinson in 1944.

men around me, but I was terribly bored with them. I wanted something much more exotic.'

It's hard to disentangle reality from fiction in anything Lesley ever said about her own life. Her seductive prose style makes her memoirs magical to read, but her relationship with the truth was nothing if not casual. With a high-flying romantic imagination, she invented and re-invented herself as she grew older, hiding some things, elaborating others, changing 'facts' as the decades passed. The question of her marriages remains an enigma: only two are official, but following a fire in her French house in 1994, she claimed to have rescued her three wedding rings. Her first recorded spouse, one Robert Bicknell, an advertising agent eleven years her senior, was about as far as you could get from exotic, but he had a delectable Georgian cottage in Richmond with a garden running down to the river, irresistible to a compulsive homemaker like Lesley. Passionately acquisitive all her life, her attachment to things was matched by her ability to wrench them from their rightful owners, a torment for any friend whose possessions she coveted. In January 1930 she married Mr Bicknell and moved into his gorgeous house, accompanied by her parents. Unequal to this assault on his territory, her husband had gone within two years. Lesley kept the house until the war. 'I too have lived in paradise', she wrote later. The man who provided the house merits no name in her memoirs.

In her nineties, she referred to Robert Bicknell as her second husband. Perhaps she had discretely followed the Traveller's advice on wedlock. A woman should marry three times, he told her: 'The first time for love, to get it out of your system. The second for money, to get it into your purse. And the third for pleasure, which has nothing to do with either love or money.' If Bicknell, married for a house, was number two, had there been a first union for love? Top of the candidates' list is the ferociously gifted Russian theatre director who dominated the British stage during the interwar years. Feodor Komisarjevsky – hypnotically attractive to women – embodied everything Lesley most prized. Light years away from the bland Englishmen who fluttered round her, he had the Slavic looks she adored, spoke seven languages and seemed to embody the Russia of her mind's eye, even tolerating her attempts to live what she saw as a Russian-style life. He ratcheted up the temperature of their affair, coming and going at will, his past shrouded in mystery. He drew her into his elite theatrical circles, meeting her secretly in Paris and introducing her to a raft of brilliant Russian émigrés, including Rachmaninov, the famous bass Chaliapin and Diaghilev, whose Ballets Russes became her latest passion. In 1932, Komisarjevsky asked her to collaborate with him on stage and costume design for his production of *The Merchant of Venice* at Stratford's new Shakespeare Memorial Theatre, a stratospheric opportunity for an inexperienced artist.

The snag to Komisarjevsky as a lover was his addiction to matrimony. He eventually notched up nine marriages, with various children along the way, ditching each bride for the next as soon as it suited him. Whether or not divorce had actually taken place made little difference. By 1934 he had discarded Lesley for the actress Peggy Ashcroft, who divorced Rupert Hart-Davis to become the eighth Mrs Komisarjevsky in 1935, shortly before she too was abandoned. Given this track record, it seems more than possible that Komisarjevsky, between or during other marriages, went through some kind of ceremony with Lesley before he left her, just another bit of marital flotsam with a ring and a few emotional scars to remember him by. She took it hard, but nearly ten years later she got her own back. Journalist Anne Scott-James, bombed out of her flat and lodging in Lesley's spare room in Swan Court, came home to find a young man in battle dress and muddy boots lying on her bed in command of the flat's only telephone. A good twelve years younger than Lesley, this was her new conquest, Feodor Komisarjevsky's son Vadim, invalided out of the army after two years and working in the film industry in London. In an earlier *Vogue* article, Lesley had described him as a stormy and single-minded individual, eager and sensitive, his burning ambition to become as good a director for film as his father had been for the stage. Lesley didn't keep him around for long, but it must have helped her settle the score.

Bombed out of her rooms in Albany during the Blitz, Lesley moved to Swan Court. It was a curious choice, the flat's unadorned modernity at odds with her fancy for the graceful decorative appeal of the eighteenth century. But with central London lodgings at a premium in wartime, an easily run flat in a good location was not to be turned down and she set about transforming flat 69's bare rooms into the stage-set Russian interior of her dreams. Colour was everywhere – in the rugs, the sensuous fabrics draped over battered Rococo settees, the mounds of embroidered cushions. With a samovar bubbling in the corner beneath her favourite icon, piles of books on floor and chairs, tables weighed down with porcelain and candelabra, now it felt like home. Chic and suited for *Vogue* meetings, her out-of-hours dress was as exotic and colourful as her interiors. Gilded mirrors threw back her reflection as she drifted about the rooms, braceleted and turbaned, dressed à la Ballets Russes in velvet jacket, silk shirt and baggy Turkish trousers, lost in dreams of Russia. Bejewelled, draped in floating rainbow silks, she lit up Swan Court's shaded courtyard like some tropical bird as she wafted out to yet another party.

And there were parties in plenty to be enjoyed in the London of the nineteen-forties. Defying the blackout, the crippling shortages and the fear of bombs, there was fun to be had in abundance. As the German army advanced, refugees in strange uniforms flooded into the city from the occupied territories of Europe and threw themselves into the whirlwind of wartime nightlife. Clubs and bars swarmed with Czechs, Norwegians, Dutchmen, dashing Polish flyers, de Gaulle's Free French supporters… a polyglot mix of exotic men ready and willing for romantic encounters. The tempo, said Lesley, was boiling, her love life – as she told Anne Scott-James – ever more rackety. Picaresque to the point of risk, said her biographer. Then one night, at a party for Free French airmen on leave in London, she spied a man with a dark Slavic face, sitting in a corner, polishing off the hostess' prized delicacy – a bowl of salted almonds. No Frenchman, she thought, hearing his 'boot-deep' voice below the wail of the saxophones, surely a genuine Russian. This is one version of their meeting, but is it true? Over the years Lesley offered others. Whatever actually happened, it was the beginning of a relationship that was to dominate her life for the better part of two decades.

Her new swain's name was, he said, Romain Gari de Kacew. This, like many other things he claimed for himself, was not entirely true. His birthplace and parentage were obscure; he spoke fluent Russian and Polish but his formative years had been spent on the move with his mother from the east – possibly Lithuania – via Warsaw towards France. By the time he was fourteen they were settled in Nice, where his mother, a lifelong and fanatical admirer of all things French, began preparing him for a brilliant career in diplomacy and literature. For Lesley, his adopted Frenchness was unimportant; as far as she was concerned he was – he had to be – Russian. How could he not be? she thought, curled in bed like a contented cat as her new lover paced the floor reciting Pushkin in his smoky bass rumble.

Besotted and needing a romantic bolt-hole for this new affair, Lesley had found a pretty top floor flat just up the road from Swan Court at 32 St. Leonard's Terrace, freezing cold but possessed of a tiny roof garden and a good supply of hot water, a comfort barely imaginable in wartime London. She stripped all traces of her Russian interior from flat 69 and decamped, leaving her friend and lodger Anne Scott-James

Lesley Blanch with husband-to-be Romain Gary, photographed by her friend Lee Miller in St. Leonard's Terrace, 1944.

in situ, gloomily contemplating the bare de-personalised space.

A year later, on April 4th 1945, Romain and Lesley were married in Chelsea Registry Office. As far as personal mythologies go, they were a well-matched pair, both given to turning fancies into facts and obscuring their pasts. (Only the night before their wedding did he tell Lesley he was Jewish.) Their marriage certificate shows Lesley shaving three years off her age, while Romain's apparently deceased father sports an invented name, nationality and occupation. Only their witnesses attended. Lesley, in love with the exotic wedding rites of the Russian Orthodox Church, thought it a banal event. Romain, moody and hypochondriacal, was making the most of a heavy, possibly psychosomatic, cold. This unpleasing occasion was a fitting start to the upheavals and disappointments that lay ahead.

Romain's glamorous foreign aura made his bride weak at the knees: his looks, his origins, his literary gifts, his dashing reputation as a fearless much-decorated wartime flyer – how could she resist him? A closer look should have told her he was hardly good husband material. Years of living in hotels with his mother had left him undomesticated, accustomed to being waited on by women and peevish when such attentions were absent. Tricky at home, often sunk in Russian gloom, he was worse when let off the leash; a compulsive womaniser, his taste ran to younger and younger girls. But his new wife, nearly ten years older, wanted both him and the life he could offer and she kept her end up, sometimes befriending his conquests and indulging in dalliances of her own during their many separations.

Two months after their marriage, Romain – now reborn as Romain Gary – published his book *Forest of Anger* in France. It shot up the bestseller lists, winning a prestigious prize and turning him overnight into a feted literary celebrity. Years later, he was to become the only writer to win the coveted Prix Goncourt twice, first for his novel *The Roots of Heaven* and later on, fraudulently under yet another identity, for *The Life Before Us*.

Romain wangled himself into the French diplomatic service and the two of them began moving from home to home, Lesley in a new manifestation as the wife *en poste*, playing the ever-charming hostess from eastern Europe to Los Angeles via Berne, New York and Mexico. One posting was to lead to more than social fripperies. Bulgaria, straddling the divide between her beloved Russia and the Orient, was then largely unknown to the West. It fired in Lesley a passion that inspired her clothes, her homes and her romantic imagination for the rest of her life. And out of this new obsession came the book, never out of print since, that was to give her a cult literary status to rival and even outclass her husband's.

The Wilder Shores of Love tells the stories of four nineteenth-century European women who had lived and loved in Arabia. Neither travellers nor explorers, these were women – like Lesley herself – lost in romantic dreams of the Orient and seeking sexual fulfilment in its erotic possibilities. It's a book in which lived experience intertwines with fact and fantasy, all expressed in unique and seductively spicy prose; surely fresh in the author's mind was the interlude when, en route for Bulgaria to join her husband, she had lingered among the glories of Istanbul to indulge herself in the arms of an ardent Turkish lover. Strong on atmosphere and insights, Lesley was less committed to historical accuracy. The book subsequently prompted scholarly research that called some of the 'facts' about her heroines into question.

Be that as it may, when *The Wilder Shores of Love* was published on September 1st 1954, it caused a sensation on both sides of the Atlantic, with 22,000 copies sold in England in the first ten days and a reprint immediately ordered in New York. Features and extracts filled the newspapers and magazines. Reviewers were impressed and enthralled. British historian and explorer Stuart Perowne declared it required reading on relations between Europeans and the Arab world. It made Lesley Blanch a feted celebrity and set the tone of her writing for the rest of her long life.

The book's success may not have helped the Gary marriage, Romain not a man to enjoy being outdone in celebrity by his spouse. They jolted along together for a few more years until Romain fell madly in love with the young actress Jean Seberg, fresh from filming Jean-Luc Godard's *À Bout de Souffle*. He and Lesley divorced in 1962 with much recrimination, which divided all their friends, Lesley refusing till the end to forgive those who kept contact with him. Anne Scott-James and her husband Macdonald Hastings gave him brief sanctuary in their Wiltshire cottage when he was writing *The Roots of Heaven*. Lesley never forgot this – to her – unacceptable favour, giving her old flatmate a frosty reception when they met briefly again years later in France. Romain finished up as the *monster-sacré* of French literature and shot himself in 1970, little more than a year after his divorced wife Jean Seberg had mysteriously been found dead in her car.

Lesley's second book took her years of travel and research, much of it in Russia and the Caucusus. *The Sabres of Paradise* is a biography of the nineteenth-century Muslim leader-prophet Imam Shamyl, whose portrait had adorned her nursery wall. It's a masterly account of Chechnya's struggle against nineteenth-century Tsarist Russia – ominously relevant to today's conflict, said *The Sunday Times* of a recent re-issue. The book was widely admired from the start and is still consulted by historians.

In the decades after her divorce from Romain Gary, Lesley made her home in France, travelled widely and wrote steadily, inspiring generations of writers, readers and critics. She published another ten books, including two on cookery, one novel and her lyrical memoir *Journey into the Mind's Eye: fragments of an autobiography*. Her final book, *Romain: un regard particulier*, published in 1998, is a memoir of life with her last husband. She remained addicted to dressing up, still in love with Arab-inspired clothes and spending the day before her hundredth birthday in search of just the right colourful headdress to mark the occasion. She died in May 2007, just short of her one hundred and third birthday, *sui generis* to the end.

MAIN SOURCES

Boston, Anne: *Lesley Blanch: Inner Landscapes, Wilder Shores*. John Murray, 2010. The definitive biography.

Scott-James, Anne: *Sketches From a Life*. Michael Joseph, 1993. Scott-James' memoir includes a vivid pen-portrait of her friend, Vogue colleague and sometime flatmate.

de Chamberet, Georgina: *On the Wilder Shores of Love: A Bohemian Life*. Virago, 2015. Blanch's writings and memoirs, edited by her goddaughter and full of personal anecdotes and insights.

By Lesley Blanch:

Journey Into The Mind's Eye: Fragments of an Autobiography. Collins, 1968. 'If you are interested in Russia – if you are interested in love – this haunting book is the one to read, and re-read. A masterpiece.' Philip Ziegler.

The Sabres of Paradise: Conquest and Vengeance in the Caucasus. John Murray, 1960.

The Wilder Shores of Love. Originally published by John Murray, in 1954. Latest edition by Simon and Schuster, 2010.

See www.lesleyblanch.com, which includes a twenty-minute broadcast Lesley Blanch made for Radio 3 in February 2007, three months before her death.

18

The *Picture Post* Pair
*Anne Eleanor Scott-James (later Lady Lancaster) (1913-2009),
Douglas Edward Macdonald 'Mac' Hastings (1909-1982)
Max (later Sir Max) Hugh MacDonald Hastings (1945-)
Flat 69 1941-1946*

W HEN JOURNALIST ANNE SCOTT-JAMES, brainy, beautiful and six feet tall, arrived in 69 Swan Court as Lesley Blanch's lodger, she'd just landed her dream job as the first women's editor of *Picture Post*, the latest weekly magazine sensation. Since 1938, when the first edition erupted onto British bookstands, the public had gone mad for its pioneering brand of photo journalism.

Staunchly liberal, anti-Fascist and populist, it reported news through the eye of the camera, its bold live-action photographs captivating readers for nearly two decades. Within two months of the launch, 1.7 million copies had flown off the shelves; three years later circulation was heading for two million.

By 1941, *Picture Post* was unquestionably the most exciting place to work in Fleet Street. Since the beginning, Anne had yearned to be part of it, although this new radical magazine could hardly have been further from the world in which she'd climbed the journalistic ladder. As Beauty Editor of *British Vogue*, commissioning glamour photographs of models and celebrities and advising readers how to present themselves on every social occasion was mostly what she did; hardly the journalistic experience to get her through the door of a provocative and edgy publication like *Picture Post*. Then, determined to escape from women's 'glossies' after war was declared, she pitched a bold idea to the editor. Run a feature about *Vogue* and I'll write you an article, she said, a daring shot in the dark that subsequently won her the offer of a job that was to last until the end of the war.

On her first day, Anne found herself with an office, a secretary and no idea what she was supposed to do. Just get on with it, she was told, so she began to explore the impact of the war on women's lives. She learnt what was wanted on the job: features had to be linked to the news and of general rather than purely female interest. Browse through the *Picture Post* archive and you can see the range of subjects she tackled – backyard farming, food preserving, women in factories, cooking with rations, childbirth in the Blitz, new treatments for war neuroses, refurbishing a bombed home, all enlivened by the superb photographs that had become the magazine's trademark. Every story had to have pictorial value. If as a writer you wanted to work alongside Bert Hardy, Leonard

Anne Scott-James, women's editor of Picture Post, training as a bus conductress in 1941 for an article on women's war work.

McCombe and the other famous *Picture Post* photographers, you had to *see* every subject before you thought of the words. Gradually, Anne said, looking at life in pictures became second nature. The glamour of her old world could be useful on occasion; when the government introduced Utility clothing, Anne chose Deborah Kerr, the nation's new favourite film star, to model the range for her piece.

Anne's colleague MacDonald Hastings – or Mac, as he was always known – was a sporty, rumbustious character and one of the big names at *Picture Post*. Tall, with a slightly donnish bespectacled look, he had a passion for field sports, a gun his accessory of choice. He'd been recruited in the first

Anne enjoys a pint, a smoke and a pin-stripe suit to illustrate the Picture Post *article 'Should Women Wear Trousers?'*

year of *Picture Post's* life as a skilled writer who specialised in country topics, a combination rare in Fleet Street but popular with readers. Early issues have Mac's articles on pheasant shooting, badger digging and otter hunting as well as farming in Britain and the lives of tramps and vets. He liked to get out and about – he wrote on crossing the Atlantic on the *Queen Mary*, crossing Canada on the Canadian Pacific Railway and buying a pair of handmade guns in London. Within a year, not yet thirty, he was one of *Picture Post's* acknowledged stars and in 1939 became the magazine's war correspondent, the perfect role for a writer of his swashbuckling inclinations. He reported from Channel convoys, destroyers and torpedo boats

The Picture Post Pair

Mac Hastings, Picture Post *war correspondent, puts on flying kit in 1944.*

with the Royal Navy, flew with Bomber Command, described the London Blitz and covered the campaign in Europe from Normandy to the Elbe, also describing these experiences in his regular BBC broadcasts. He relished the occasions when he had to sign a 'blood chit', a document that absolved the armed forces from any responsibility for what happened to him on operations. He became known for bravery and occasional recklessness on the battlefield, a reputation backed up by firsthand accounts from his *Picture Post* photographer colleagues. Matched with brilliant photographs, this was journalism of the highest calibre. *Picture Post's* writers were usually credited in small print at the end of the copy. Now the pieces had star billing, Mac's byline at the head.

'I'm going to marry that girl', Mac told his colleagues when he saw a photograph of *Picture Post's* beautiful, willowy women's editor. And so began his long campaign for Anne's hand. The first shot was in the summer of 1941, when he asked her to contribute to his weekly BBC broadcast to America, 'London Letter'. Introducing her on air, he told listeners that she looked as if she'd just stepped out of an advertisement, with the peaches-and-cream complexion that men talk about and women envy. 'She's as high as my heart, or higher,' he said, 'and the nicest girl that ever held a man's hand under the Bomber's Moon I've written about...' Anne followed this romantic and very public declaration by telling the audience that what she loved was her garden, and the delights of digging and sowing and planting and pruning.

Among Anne's previous sentimental encounters had been another rather wild man who loved guns. In 1939 she'd been married very briefly to a raffish journalist called Derek Verschoyle, literary editor of *The Spectator*. A hard-drinking clubbable character, he kept a rifle in his office, sitting with feet on desk, potting cats through the window and practising his target skills on the garden wall. He'd been taught at his Welsh prep school by Evelyn Waugh, who used him in his novel *Decline and Fall* as a model for the frighteningly precocious schoolboy Peter Beste-Chetwynde. Waugh, though completely ignorant of the instrument, had to teach Verschoyle to play the organ, a real-life experience that found its way into the novel. No doubt Verschoyle, like Beste-Chetwynde, left school better at mixing a good dry martini than employing the vox humana or the diapason. Anne and Verschoyle divorced after less than a year. He went on to become a spy and a publisher and had four more wives. She wrote him immediately out of her life, only allowing him a tiny look-in, when she was ninety, in her *Who's Who* entry.

Anne has left no description of what she did to flat 69 after Lesley Blanch's departure, commenting simply that when Lesley's Russian exotica was removed, all remnants of personality went with it, the space left plain and unadorned. But Swan Court was a practical place to lay one's head after work, and maybe Anne did little other than the elegant arrangement of her collection of fine family china; her real love – and Mac's – was always the Berkshire cottage she'd bought before the war and kept for a lifetime. In 1943, Mac, now installed in the flat, proposed marriage with the unsettling declaration 'I mean to hook you', a somewhat violent fishing metaphor that she said later should have made her doubt his matrimonial suitability. In early June 1944, like many other Swan Court couples before and after, they were married in Chelsea Registry Office, the honeymoon in the cottage lasting for just two days before Mac was sent off to cover the Normandy landings. Anne commented later that wedlock had begun bumpily but Mac seemed cheerful enough, often telling people that he now had the three things he'd wanted most – a Churchill gun, a Hardy rod and a beautiful wife. This statement of ownership and priorities was strongly and justifiably resented by his new bride. As for many other couples wed in wartime, the extent of their incompatibility began to emerge when peace came. They clashed over everything, from politics and private passions to friends and holidays – Mac right-wing and adoring guns, field sports and deer-stalking, she liberal and art-loving, her ideal holiday a church crawl in France.

At the end of the war, Anne left *Picture Post* for a six-year stint as editor of *Harper's Bazaar*. She was the youngest editor in London, with a high-profile job and her first baby, her to-do lists veering from the planning of features for the next issue to the buying of Chilprufe vests in Hayfords. The advent of a full-time nanny prompted the move from Swan Court to a larger flat in Kensington, and after her second child, she left *Harper's* to write a book. *In the Mink* is a memoir, loosely disguised as a novel, about her time in the fashion business. It was well received by readers, less so by the thinly veiled characters she described, the cruellest piece a brilliant but deeply condescending portrait based on the family's devoted nanny, and read by all her fellow nannies as they pushed their prams together in Kensington Gardens. Unsurprisingly, Nanny Hastings never felt the same after that about her employer, but stuck it out until the children were grown.

Writing of his mother after her death, Max Hastings paints a vibrant and rather intimidating picture of Anne Scott-James. Dauntingly tall, he said, with the habit of command and an absolute intolerance of fools, never less than flawlessly turned out and seldom at a loss for the *mot juste*, often acidulous. Difficult attributes in a mother and an employer, certainly, and few other Swan Court residents could have outfaced her each morning as she strode across the courtyard on her way to Fleet Street, top-to-toe couture and perfect make-up, every hair in place, manicured hand on elegant hat under the draughty archways. Perhaps she wasn't always as confident as she seemed. Surprisingly, this formidably intelligent and perfect woman could admit to feeling inadequate; lumbering and coarse in perception, she said, when in the company of her country neighbour, the writer Rosamond Lehmann, and conversationally outgunned by her mercurial colleague and flatmate Lesley Blanch.

On the night of Monday December 31st 1945 Mac Hastings sat down on his own in flat 69 to write, seal and store away a long letter to his three-day-old son. It tells small Max of the writers in his family background, his parents' careers, the state of the post-war world into which he had just been born, and that his mother was regarded as one of the most beautiful women in London. A rather touching piece, it was given to Max Hastings on his twenty-first birthday and seems to indicate a steady affection rarely to be seen in his exciting but unpredictable parent. Max wrote later that his father was more often observed going rather than coming, always off to shoots, to fishing expeditions, to assignments or to his London Club, the Savage. Frequently working abroad, Mac's returns brought a shower of presents from exotic places – a cowboy suit, model soldiers, dozens of toy guns, Bedouin robes, the hoof of a bison he'd shot in India.

Mac had what his small son saw as superhuman powers to make everything exciting. Pictures taken of him on foreign assignments certainly seem to indicate a romantic, almost childish, love of dressing-up. He figures as a Bedouin on a camel in Jordan, a snake charmer complete with turban and cobra in India, a lasso-clutching cowboy in Alberta, and in cap and goggles learning to fly a Tiger Moth. But most thrilling of all to a small boy who longed to emulate his father were the guns. Mac's huge collection of antique and modern weapons and ammunition was never locked up, leading to several risky incidents in the country when his gun-mad son, having perfected the stripping and reassembling of the various weapons, decided to start firing them. A near-disastrous apogee was achieved on the occasion when Max, disturbed by a rumour that all World War II weapons would be removed from circulation, smuggled his favourite pistol plus ammunition back to the London flat. Then, watching the American TV drama *Perry Mason* while stripping and reassembling the pistol, he managed to fire it at the television, which exploded in smoke and showers of glass. The ensuing family row, even by Hastings standards, was judged a corker.

The Hastings' marriage dragged on uncompanionably until 1962 when they divorced. In their last years together,

Mac became a heavy drinker, increasingly morose when in his cups. Anne withdrew into what her son described as a cloud of contempt and eventually gave him the push. The family split in two: daughter Clare remaining with her mother; Max, then seventeen, staying alongside his father. Mother and son were on frosty terms, seeing little or nothing of each other for many years. In 1967 Anne remarried very happily to the cartoonist, writer and theatre designer Sir Osbert Lancaster, a surprising union given his admission that she had terrified him at first. She was, he said, 'so elegant, so aloof and so much taller than me'. This was nothing new: before her second marriage Anne had always chased love in a series of relationships that went nowhere, her liking for men matched by her ability to frighten the life out of many of them.

Despite personal upheavals, Anne's career changed and flourished. With stints at the *Sunday Express*, *Beaverbrook Newspapers*, and to great acclaim as a *Daily Mail* columnist, over the years her brand of pioneering journalism radically changed the way women's interests were covered in the press. From 1968 she worked as a freelance journalist, broadcaster and in television, becoming a household name admired for her gardening expertise on air and in print, publishing nine books on flowers, gardens and gardening over twenty years and a volume of autobiography when she was eighty. Much saddened by Osbert's death in 1986, she soldiered on for another twenty-three years, elegant and sharp as a tack, reading Virgil in Latin and Flaubert in French to pass the time in her retirement home. Brave, blunt and spiky to the end, she died in 2009 aged ninety-six.

After eighteen months more or less alone with the gin bottle, Mac Hastings remarried. His new wife, sixteen years younger and the widow of his publisher Michael Joseph, combined a practical take on domestic life with a saintly disposition, coping with her husband's alcoholic bouts and giving birth to their daughter Harriet. Mac's career went steadily downhill. In the nineteen-fifties he'd become a household name in television; now his contempt for the changing times and the new faces coming up in the world of broadcasting combined with his gin habit to make him unemployable. Producers joked that if you wanted him to do a piece to camera after lunch, you'd be wise to provide a doorpost for him to lean against while doing it. By 1965 his BBC contract had run out. Bankrolled by his wife, now chairman of Michael Joseph, he made the occasional documentary and continued to turn out books, which sold poorly. The glory days were over, a very real talent thrown away. He died in 1982 aged seventy-two, leaving family, friends and old colleagues with a bagful of mixed memories. Tom Hopkinson, his old editor at *Picture Post*, called him 'a most lovable man, all the more so for his irascibility that often dissolved into laughter and his carefully cherished prejudices.' The BBC was unrepresented at his funeral.

MAIN SOURCES

Blanch, Lesley: *Journey Into The Mind's Eye: Fragments of an Autobiography*. Collins, 1968.

Hastings, Max: *Did You Really Shoot the Television?: A Family Fable*. Harper Press, 2010.

Scott-James, Anne: *Sketches From a Life*. Michael Joseph, 1993. Autobiography, written in the form of an extended letter to her daughter Clare.

Whitehorn, Katharine: Essay in *The Oxford Dictionary of National Biography*, January 10th 2013.

See also by Anne Scott-James: *In the Mink* (1952), *Down to Earth* (1971),

Sissinghurst: The Making of a Garden (1974), *The Pleasure Garden: An Illustrated History of British Gardening* (with Sir Osbert Lancaster) (1977), *The Cottage Garden* (1981), *Glyndebourne: The Gardens* (with Christopher Lloyd) (1983), *Perfect Plant, Perfect Garden* (1987), *Gardening Letters to my Daughter* (1991).

19
Crime's Queen and her Consort
*Dame Agatha Mary Clarissa Christie
(Lady Mallowan) DBE (1890-1976)
Sir Max Edgar Lucien Mallowan CBE
(1904-1978)
Flat 48 1947-1976*

WITH SALES OF HER CRIME FICTION NUDGING fifty million and an international reputation, Agatha Christie came to Swan Court with her second husband Max Mallowan towards the end of the most creative period of her writing life. Flat 48, which she owned until her death, was to be one of the most enduring acquisitions in her lifelong love affair with property. Ashfield in Torquay, the scene of her never-to-be-forgotten late-Victorian childhood, was the first home she fell in love with; in adult life she amused herself by buying and refurbishing run-down houses, briefly or intermittently living in some, and letting or re-selling as the mood took her. At one time between the wars she owned eight properties, only parting with them with great reluctance. In the post-war years, three in her portfolio endured: the beautiful Greenway overlooking the river Dart in Devon, Winterbrook House near Wallingford in Oxfordshire with its garden running down to the Thames, and, from the end of 1947, Swan Court's flat 48.

At heart peripatetic, Agatha moved regularly between her homes throughout the year. After her second marriage she also made annual winter visits to the Middle East, where she joined in her husband's archaeological excavations, helping to restore ancient artefacts and using her Pond's Cold Cream for cleaning ivories. The winter of 1947/48 was no exception; hardly had she taken over the keys to flat 48 than she and Max were off for their first post-war visit to Iraq. Travel did not hinder her writing, the 'Christie for Christmas' insisted on by her publishers often accompanied by short story collections and stage adaptations. A life of constant domestic upheaval – which would have done for many another writer – was as nothing to the Queen of Crime. What she was working on was kept private, the next plot always in her head but never discussed. At the various 'dig houses' and at Winterbrook, she just slipped away from everyone, shut the door and got on with it. Greenway she kept for Devon summers with the family; Swan Court was for short London visits to meet her publishers, see friends and go to the theatre.

A pretty girl with a good figure and a waterfall of pale blonde hair, the young Agatha Miller grew up with her American father and English mother in a large comfortable house on the outskirts of Torquay, then an elegant and fashionable seaside resort. Energetically pursued by the young men of the neighbourhood, on the eve of the First World War she fell wildly in love with Archie Christie, a young army officer with a passion for aeroplanes who was about to join the Royal Flying Corps. They married on Christmas Eve 1914 and spent the next four years largely apart, Archie serving in France, where he was mentioned several times in despatches and, in 1918, awarded the Distinguished Service Order (DSO). Agatha spent the war working in the Torquay Hospital, first as a volunteer and subsequently as a qualified dispenser. During this time she wrote her first detective story, a dispensary full of poisons the perfect environment for meditating on murder.

In the post-war years, the Christies settled into married life, at first in London and then in Archie's ideal – the Surrey suburbs with a golf course nearby. For Agatha, with her background of beaches and the wild Devon countryside, this was an alien place. But her life was changing – the ten years from 1919 saw her first book deal and her gradual transformation from an occasional contributor to magazines and newspapers to a best-selling professional author. She had also, to her misery, become well-known, and by the end of the decade, her natural dislike of the limelight was to overwhelm her in an episode not entirely explained to this day.

The famous 'disappearance' had its origins at the beginning of 1926 when the Christies' marriage was in the doldrums. They had bought Styles, a large suburban villa in Sunningdale, handy for Archie's commute to London and the golf course where he spent an increasing amount of time. Agatha found the house depressing and, with the need for servants and two cars, money was a constant problem. That year her mother died and she spent time at the old family home in Torquay tidying up her affairs. Archie stayed at his club in London and spent his weekends playing golf. Then in August he told Agatha he'd fallen in love with Nancy Neele, a family acquaintance, and wanted a divorce. They staggered on through the autumn, Agatha distraught, trying to work, eating too little and sleeping badly. Then on Friday December 3rd, around 11pm, she got into her car, drove off into the night and disappeared. The next morning the car was found abandoned some miles away at Newlands Corner near Guildford.

For the next ten days, every newspaper in the country carried banner headlines charting the search for the famous novelist. Styles was besieged by journalists, the Christies' small daughter Rosalind escorted to school by police officers. Sightings came in from readers all over the country. When Archie arrived with the police to identify the car, a huge crowd had gathered, attended by vans selling food and drink. Hundreds of police searched the area and the ponds were dragged. On December 12th, the police organised what the *Evening News* called 'The Great Sunday Hunt for Mrs Christie', with members of the public asked to put on stout clothes and bring any handy bloodhounds to help search the thick bracken-covered ground around Newlands Corner. No body was found and the speculation grew. The Home Secretary pressed the police to step up the search. The papers offered rewards. The 'experts' pontificated. Suicide, murder, mental breakdown, revenge on her errant husband, amnesia – or even a publicity stunt? The world knew Mrs Christie as a writer of fearsome ingenuity: someone who could play a trick on her readers – as she had famously done in *The Murder of Roger Ackroyd* – was surely capable of any kind of deception.

Then on December 14th, Agatha was tracked down to the Hydropathic Hotel in Harrogate, where she had been staying quietly since December 4th, bizarrely using the surname of her husband's mistress. Archie went to fetch her. Mobbed by journalists at the hotel, they were followed to Harrogate station and chased down the platform onto the train in a press feeding-frenzy that continued when they reached London. It was an experience that gave an already shy young woman a lifelong fear and distrust of journalists; she rarely gave press interviews and was almost incapable of speaking in public. Years later, in 1956, the actress Mary Law, appearing in Christie's stage adaptation of *Toward Zero*, recalled the author as painfully shy and ill at ease socially, although vocal enough when it came to actors who deviated from her dialogue.

Agatha herself never wrote or spoke publicly about the episode and, over ninety years on, the story runs and runs, in books, articles and on screen. In 1979, Vanessa Redgrave starred in a film about the episode. Twenty years later, Jared Cade wrote his own account, claiming that she disappeared on purpose. Andrew Norman, in 2006, suggested a 'fugue state' of temporary and reversible amnesia. A year later, Christie's most recent biographer, Laura Thompson, thought it all brought on by shock and best left unexplained. Gillian Flynn's 2012 novel *Gone Girl* and its subsequent film bear many resemblances to the Christie disappearance. And today in Harrogate, the Hydropathic – now renamed The Old Swan – still jumps on the Christie bandwagon, its brochure encouraging guests to dine in the famous glass-ceilinged Wedgwood Restaurant, where for ten days in 1926 the famous writer sat unrecognised, doing her crossword at a table for one.

The first two years after this mysterious happening were tough, with the divorce finalised and Archie's marriage to Nancy Neele. But Agatha the writer kept on going and with a new agent, a new publisher and impressively raised royalties, the next two decades were to be the most productive of her career. No longer the suburban wife, her horizons expanded, and in the spring of 1929, she joined the archaeologist Leonard

Dame Agatha Christie in comfortable matronhood with Max Mallowan, photographed for The Sphere *magazine in 1946.*

Woolley and his wife Katharine for the digging season at Ur in southern Mesopotamia, where she met the young Max Mallowan, a trainee archaeologist working as Woolley's assistant. Knowledgeable and a good Arabist, Max was instructed to show their distinguished visitor the excavations. The two of them got on well from the start, Agatha enthusiastic about the dig and enjoying Max's company as they travelled together back to Baghdad. This entertaining trip included an impromptu bathe in a sparkling salt lake, Agatha modestly wrapped in a pink silk vest and two pairs of knickers.

In later years Max Mallowan seemed the true blue English intellectual, tweeded and pipe-smoking, comfortable at home in his book-lined study. His antecedents were far from this, his duelling-scarred soldier father of Slav and Austrian stock, his Parisienne mother the daughter of an opera singer. Catholic via his mother but far from devout, he emerged from Lancing School and Oxford ambitious, charming and skilled in the art of pleasing the right people. Leonard and Katharine Woolley had been important conquests, setting his foot firmly on the archaeological ladder; now the lonely, likeable and much older Mrs Christie offered a prize of a different kind. He established himself as an amusing and helpful companion and friend, meeting up with her in London, staying with her in Devon, making himself quietly indispensable. And in September 1930 they were married in Edinburgh, altering their ages on the certificate to show a gap of six, rather than fourteen, years.

Although, for Agatha, marriage to Max Mallowan was based on the mutual friendship and shared interests she had never found with Archie Christie, not everyone approved of it. Some, like Agatha's sister Madge and her husband, thought the young bridegroom a fortune hunter, perhaps inevitable when an ambitious young man in his mid-twenties marries a very wealthy woman nearing her fortieth birthday. Certainly for him it was a good move, his new financial independence enabling him to abandon the demanding Woolleys and pursue his own career throughout the nineteen-thirties. As an acknowledged expert in Western Asiatic archaeology, the post-war years brought him prestigious work and academic recognition, his knighthood in 1968 followed eight years later by an emeritus fellowship at All Souls College, Oxford. He and Agatha seem to have jogged along contentedly enough, the only blip on the marital horizon the occasional queries about Max's relationship with his assistant and epigraphist Barbara

Parker, including the story – never verified – that they had been caught *in flagrante* in flat 48. Whatever the truth, within a year of Agatha's death, Barbara Parker became the second Lady Mallowan.

Agatha Christie was fifty-seven when she arrived in Swan Court, a household name as a novelist and playwright and now in comfortable matronhood, her hair iron-grey and her fancy for thick tweed suits doing little to hide an ever-expanding waistline. Visiting me in Swan Court in 2018, her grandson Mathew Prichard talked about staying in flat 48 when he was growing up. He remembered his bedroom overlooking the courtyard and the flat's large comfortable sitting room with its four windows facing Flood Street, the walls hung with his grandmother's favourite paintings, including a Paul Nash. The two of them often ate in the Swan Court restaurant under the watchful eye of its autocratic manageress Betty, Agatha revelling in the rich veal and egg dishes that often figured on the menu. Agatha was often to be seen lunching with her old friend Sybil Thorndike, the two Dames happily swapping theatrical gossip over creamed chicken and rice. Betty's favourites among the older Swan Court residents could do no wrong, but when Mathew arrived one day minus grandmother but plus three undergraduate friends, suddenly, despite an empty restaurant, there was no table available.

Agatha's passions had matured with her, for decorating houses, for gardens, for travel and for food – herself no mean cook. Culinary descriptions sprinkle the pages of her autobiography: lobsters, mounds of caviar, rich sauces, rice puddings, and her favourite drink, a glass of milk diluted half and half with thick cream. Food pops up again and again in her detective stories. Miss Marple's housekeeper is famous for her scones. Hercule Poirot deplores the English breakfast and loves his little pots of chocolate. Always immaculate in dress, Poirot draws his valet's attention to a mark on his waistcoat precisely identified as a *morceau* of the *filet de sole à la Jeanette* enjoyed the day before in the Ritz. But it's not only the detectives who love what's on their plate; a jewel thief, about to snaffle some world-famous rubies, prepares himself with a pre-work dinner of *omelette fines herbes*, steak Béarnaise and *Savarin au Rhum*. And if there's a killing in the house, you can expect the menus to suffer. After the murder of a house guest, the cook fears the upset will have affected the lightness of her pastry. At lunch, after a body has been found beside the swimming pool, the hostess praises her cook's tact in serving caramel custard, a confection only quite enjoyed by the family: 'There would be something gross, after the death of a friend, in eating one's favourite pudding.'

Christie fanatics relish such light-hearted details alongside their reverence for her plots and her supreme skill at manipulating her readers with a trail of carefully planted clues and red herrings. But it's not all adulation. Christie books are as despised by some as they are revered by others. Detractors cite the woodenness of her characters, the artificiality of her settings, the inadequacy of her prose when compared to the likes of Margery Allingham and Dorothy Sayers. Well-known names on both sides have joined the fray. Bernard Levin did his best to close *The Mousetrap* on the grounds that such an inferior play should not be clogging up an important West End theatre. His campaign in the press backfired, causing a run on seats by people who wanted to see what all the fuss was about. T.S. Eliot and Evelyn Waugh were fans, as was the classical scholar Maurice Bowra, said to have re-read the Christie oeuvre every year. On occasions, Dylan Thomas felt that poetry was not the only thing in life, saying he'd sooner lie in a hot bath, reading Agatha Christie and sucking sweets. More recently, the French author, filmmaker and poet

Michel Houellebecq became an admirer. The biographer and columnist AN Wilson calls Christie a genius, while some crime writers, like Julian Symons, have taken every opportunity to snipe. However, as Wilson has pointed out, Christie's sales – now over a billion in English and another billion in translation – may provoke a degree of professional envy.

All but the most devoted admirer would agree that the Christie oeuvre is patchy, the huge output – sixty-six novels and fourteen short story collections – containing good reads alongside pot-boilers. The twenty years prior to her arrival in Swan Court saw the best of her work; paradoxically, the decline of her powers in the following decades was accompanied by a dramatic increase in her fame, largely for stage and screen adaptations. First off in the forties came the stage version of *And Then There Were None*, followed by René Clair's film. When her stage adaptation of one of her best books, *The Hollow*, opened in the West End in 1951, her agent Edmund Cork said it almost burst the Fortune Theatre. In 1952, *The Mousetrap* – still playing sixty-seven years later – preceded the success of *Witness for the Prosecution*, which packed out every performance in London and New York and was followed by Billy Wilder's film, a raging hit starring Charles Laughton, Tyrone Power and Marlene Dietrich.

Golden years indeed, but the phenomenal success was blighted by increasing financial anxiety. Despite huge sales and royalties larger than those paid to Bernard Shaw, Agatha was often short of money – British supertax rates were crippling and the US revenue pursued her for back tax on her American earnings. Disentangling it all was a long and complicated affair that dragged on for years, the difference between what she earned and what she retained a constant puzzle. 'Where is it all?' she implored her agent.

In the New Year's Honours for 1971, Agatha Christie

was made a Dame Commander of the British Empire. She was eighty years old and at the height of her fame. She'd continued writing into old age, publishing her last book *Postern of Fate* in 1973 to good reviews and sales in Britain and America. She outlived her most famous creation, Hercule Poirot, whose death she had recorded earlier in *Curtain*, which was eventually published in 1975. She died at Winterbrook House in January 1976, aged eighty-six, and is buried nearby in Cholsey. Max Mallowan died two years later.

MAIN SOURCES

Christie, Agatha: *An Autobiography*. Collins, 1977.
Christie, Agatha: *Come, Tell Me How You Live*. Collins, 1946. Max Mallowan's work in Syria, described by his wife.
Keating, HRE (ed): *Agatha Christie: First Lady of Crime*. Weidenfeld and Nicolson, 1977.
Mallowan, Max: *Nimrud and its Remains*. Collins, 1966.
Mallowan, Max: *Twenty-five Years of Mesopotamian Discovery*. Collins, 1956
Morgan, Janet: *Agatha Christie: A Biography*. Collins, 1984.
Osborne, Charles: *The Life and Crimes of Agatha Christie*. Harper Collins, 1999.
Thompson, Laura: *Agatha Christie: An English Mystery*. Headline Review, 2007.

20

The Newly-Weds
Denis (later Sir Denis) Thatcher MBE
(1915-2003)
Margaret Hilda (later Baroness)
Thatcher (1925-2013)
Flat 112 1947-1957

W‌HEN DENIS THATCHER, LOVER OF FLASHY sports cars and rugby football, arrived in Swan Court, he was nursing a broken heart after the ending of his wartime marriage. Three years later he brought home a second bride, just twenty-six years old, with a good pair of legs – as he said – plus vaulting political ambition and a fancy for flamboyant hats.

It all began with a blind dinner date on a frosty evening in February 1949. The Dartford Conservatives were holding a meeting to choose a new candidate to stand in the next election, and their eye had fallen on a pert keen-as-mustard young hopeful from Grantham called Margaret Roberts. Denis Thatcher, shy and a bit of a misogynist, had been persuaded by a work colleague to meet her at dinner afterwards. It proved inspired match-making. Margaret, not long out of Oxford and working as a research chemist, was in the starting blocks of a political career that would dominate her life. Denis admired her intelligence and vigorous, against-all-the-odds approach to campaigning. What she lacked in life experience, he could provide; at thirty-five, he was twelve years older, public-school educated and running his family business. He had independent means, a classy car and a fashionable flat in Chelsea – perfect for a small-town girl on her way up.

A promising match it may have been, but it was hardly a whirlwind affair. Asked years later if it had been love at

Margaret Roberts in her favourite hat, canvassing in October 1951.

first sight, Margaret denied it. At the time, she told her sister that on first meeting Denis she thought him a perfect gent, shy and reserved, quite nice but not a frightfully attractive creature. As for marriage, she had two elections to fight first, she said. Denis too was busy, much taken up with running Atlas, the Thatcher family's paint and preservative business, and developing his skills as a rugby football referee. For over two years they pursued a mild courtship, dining out from time to time in London, their social life revolving around Margaret's political meetings and the regular – but hardly romantic –National Paint Federation dinners. Interviewed by Margaret's biographer, Charles Moore, Denis recalled the day in the autumn of 1951 when, just returned from a bachelor holiday in France, he proposed to Margaret in the Swan Court flat. She took a while to accept, her immediate concern the forthcoming election: she feared that if it were known she was to be married, voters would question her ability to pursue a serious political career. On the other hand, she enjoyed Denis' company, he shared her political views and, appealingly, he could promise her financial security. She eventually gave in, with the proviso that the news be kept under wraps during the election campaign. On October 24th, the eve of polling day, the engagement was leaked to the press. It was Margaret's second shot at the Dartford seat. Once again she lost, but once again she had reduced the Labour majority.

With the engagement official, there followed a rather sticky visit to Margaret's parents in Grantham. At first neither Alfred Roberts, a prosperous grocer and devout Methodist, or his wife were sure about their prospective son-in-law. A divorcé, they thought, lives in Chelsea, and as for that sports car... Then Margaret noticed that Denis, fond of the bottle, was getting restive. 'Denis does like a drink, Father,' she said.

Alfred came up to scratch after blowing the dust off a very old bottle of sherry.

They were married on December 13th 1951 at Wesley's Chapel in City Road, Denis noting that his father-in-law probably thought the venue halfway to Rome. The bride wore sapphire-blue velvet, chosen to keep out the cold and topped off by a jaunty off-the-face hat with ostrich feathers curling down one side, a favourite design copied from one she'd worn as Parliamentary candidate. The reception was held at 5 Carlton Gardens, the grand Nash house owned by Margaret's political mentor Sir Alfred Bossom, MP for Maidstone. The bridegroom failed to make a speech, claiming he didn't know it was expected, a curious lapse for a man who'd been married before. Then it was off to Madeira for the honeymoon, a

Dressed in blue velvet to keep out the cold, Margaret leaves the church with Denis after their wedding on December 13th 1951.

somewhat underwhelming experience described by Denis afterwards as 'quite pleasant'. They undertook what he called 'a sort of economic survey', watching lace-making and touring a wine company. On the journey home Margaret was devastatingly seasick.

The young Mrs Thatcher who arrived in Swan Court in the new year was the epitome of a pinny-wearing nineteen-fifties' housewife, rigidly schooled in domestic economy at her mother's knee. Flat 112 was large and three-bedroomed, its sitting room overlooking Flood Street and complete with big cherry-red sofas and walls covered in Denis' favourite Bateman cartoons. The new bride approached running the household with the same organised attack she would use to such effect in her political life, prudent management always at the top of the agenda as she shopped, baked, cleaned and re-organised. Marriage to a wealthy man did not dent her inborn thrift, a coveted Royal Doulton tea and dinner service purchased with sixpenny pieces saved up in a jar. Denis seems to have borne up well under her assault on his domestic arrangements, even when his comfortable bachelor eccentricities came under scrutiny. On one occasion Margaret, her eye perhaps on a Sunday roast, found no bottom shelf in the oven. Denis explained he hadn't needed one: 'It's where I keep the gin.'

Margaret's skills at household management extended to her wardrobe. Choosing, making and altering clothes, as taught by her seamstress mother, was an essential and pleasurable task, bordering on obsession. From her teens onwards, the dozens of letters she wrote to her older sister Muriel tell of shopping trips and what she wore on dates. She writes of where she bought her undies, their colour and trimming, the fabric and style of her dresses, the jewellery and hats she wore and the bags she carried. Outfits had to match the occasion, her favourite look classic and tailored, time spent choosing just the right accessories. As she fought over the years to establish herself in a world belonging almost exclusively to men, this emphasis on the art of feminine presentation was to serve her well. Clothes played their part when she eventually won her nomination as candidate for Finchley: her 'striking appearance' in smart black coatdress and matching hat provided a pleasing contrast to her main rival, a local one-legged brigadier.

That was all in the future as she settled into her new routine in Swan Court, politics briefly taking a back seat. Opting to read for the Bar, she plunged into an intensive law course. Married life seemed to have interfered little with old habits, Denis still dividing his time between the office, his refereeing and socialising with his old schoolmates, she studying, speaking from time to time at Conservative events and as driven as ever. Then motherhood loomed; by the end of the year she was pregnant, the baby due in September 1953.

It was a difficult pregnancy. Margaret was unwell much of the time, and in mid-August she was rushed to hospital to be told she was expecting twins. They were born by Caesarean section, weighing four pounds each. As she contemplated her new son and daughter, Margaret revelled in the safe arrival of an instant complete family and the knowledge that she need never be pregnant again. Denis, unaware of any of this, was happily celebrating England's Ashes victory at the Oval. Later at the hospital, possibly a bit the worse for wear, he took a cursory look at the two tiny wrinkled infants: 'My God, they look like rabbits,' he said. 'Put them back.'

In her biography of her father, Carol Thatcher wrote that she and Mark had been born to two extraordinary people, but that didn't necessarily make them extraordinary parents. Certainly Denis wasn't that enthusiastic at the beginning. As for Margaret, she added motherhood to the list of household chores to be undertaken alongside her career, and whiled away her two weeks in hospital after the births studying law and sorting out the application for her Bar finals.

The Margaret of this era was, as her daughter wrote later, a superwoman long before the epithet was coined. She juggled working, studying, organising the household, cooking, sewing, ironing and planning each day's routine for the twins. By now, with a live-in nanny, the expanded household needed more space, so the Thatchers rented the flat next door and joined the two together. By December, Margaret had finished her law studies, qualified and started at the Bar, joining chambers in the Inner Temple. 'Mrs Thatcher was always the ambitious one,' recalled their nanny. 'She set her sights very high and got her own way because Mr Thatcher allowed her to.' Each day she set off to work, mind on the job, often forgetting to turn and wave to her children watching from the window. Denis, in general not much connected to his small twins, won the nanny's approval by nearly always remembering.

Reflecting later on her childhood, their daughter said that neither of her parents could be described as natural or comfortable with young children. They both disliked family holidays, Denis arranging annual business trips abroad for the month of August, Margaret depositing the twins at the seaside with the nanny and returning to work. As her career in public life blossomed, Margaret was always quick to explain how efficiently she combined politics and family to the detriment of neither. A driven workaholic not naturally attracted to the joys of motherhood, she knew she would vegetate at the kitchen sink all day. She insisted that her family did not suffer at all through her political ambitions. This was of course a fiction, something her biographer Charles Moore says she later realised. Denis too came to regret time not spent with his children as they grew up.

The Newly-Weds

At the end of 1954, Margaret, now a well-regarded young barrister, asked Conservative Central Office to remove her name from the list of potential candidates. This change of heart didn't last long; a year later, the law having failed to capture her heart and soul, she was feeling the temptation to return to politics. In 1957 the Thatchers left Swan Court for Kent, and Margaret was back on the candidates list. After more unsuccessful shots at adoption, including Hemel Hempstead and Maidstone, she struck lucky in Finchley in July 1958, beating her rival Thomas Langton by forty-six votes to forty-three at the final selection meeting. It was a close-run result, but she may not have known that it was also fraudulent. The Conservative chairman, Bertie Blatch, keen to get her into the seat and knowing her rival would have a good chance elsewhere, admitted privately to manipulating the count to give her the edge. After Margaret had presented herself to the press and the voters of Finchley at her adoption meeting two weeks later, the leader writer on the *Finchley Press* congratulated the Conservatives for having armed themselves with a new weapon – a clever woman; an unsurprising compliment, given that the newspaper was owned by Bertie Blatch. Denis Thatcher, in Africa on a business trip, had missed yet another significant event in his wife's career. Staggering, rather drunk, onto a plane in Nigeria, he found a copy of the *Evening Standard*. On an inside page was a small article headlined 'Tories Choose Beauty'.

Blatch's shenanigans in Margaret's favour were to prove an astute political move for the party when it came to the general election of October 1959. Sir Keith Joseph, who became Margaret's greatest political ally, said that anyone could have guessed her likely success. The constituency was a moderately prosperous, petit-bourgeois, owner-occupied suburban constituency and a safe Tory seat, ideal for her. She and Finchley were both upwardly mobile. She was thirty-four years old, good-looking, well-dressed, and a speaker of compelling political force. She romped home with a majority of over sixteen thousand.

Was Denis Thatcher, proudly celebrating his wife's success, prepared for what lay ahead for them both? Sixteen years later she would become leader of the Tory Opposition; four years after that the two of them were in Downing Street. Advising and supporting behind the scenes as she made her way up the ladder was one thing, but to a shy man, the prospect of a career as two-steps-behind consort to a Prime Minister must have been daunting. As he pointed out, he had to un-shy himself pretty damn quick. Margaret was quick to acknowledge her debt to him, saying later that he had been a fund of shrewd advice and penetrating comment, which he had sensibly saved for her rather than the outside world. 'He gives me a sense of

Denis and Margaret, now Leader of the Opposition, wave to the media from the doorway of 19 Flood Street, 1975.

perspective. If I have done something silly, we talk about it and he makes me see sense.' John Major, who succeeded Margaret Thatcher as Prime Minister, thought Denis a substantial man in his own right: 'He provided (his wife) with dispassionate advice that he was wise enough to keep private and she was wise enough to accept.' Discretion was the name of the game for Denis and no hardship; he regarded journalists as 'reptiles' and never gave media interviews. When Margaret hit the top rung in 1975, becoming leader of the Opposition, the media besieged the latest Thatcher home at 19 Flood Street, just across the road from their old Swan Court flat. Denis, by then a director of Burmah Oil, was noticeably cool under fire. He good-humouredly posed for photographs but was back at his desk at nine the next morning as though nothing had happened.

On May 15th 1979, soon after Margaret Thatcher had arrived in Downing Street, the satirical magazine *Private Eye* published the first of a series of letters entitled 'Dear Bill'. They purported to come from Denis; 'Bill' was always assumed to be Bill Deedes, columnist, Cabinet minister and editor of *The Daily Telegraph*. The letters, sublime parodies of an old buffer's blimpish opinions and turn of phrase, appeared every fortnight until Denis Thatcher's death twenty-four years later. The writers, John Wells and Richard Ingrams, portrayed Denis as outrageous in his lack of political correctness, appalled by bores encountered at Downing Street, and frank in his longing for a round of golf and several gins. The characterisation was not entirely fictitious. When the letter-writer branded the Labour Party 'Commies' and described the BBC as 'that nest of Pinkoes and Traitors at Shepherd's Bush', the humour was exaggerated but certainly not a complete invention. Margaret was unamused by the whole thing; daughter Carol remarked at how often the letters got it right. 'Dear Bill' made Denis Thatcher a gently mocked national treasure.

The Grantham grocer's daughter who had made it to one of the world's top jobs never relinquished the basic values of thrift and efficiency that she had brought with her as a young bride to Swan Court. She remained firm in the belief that a woman who could understand the problems of running a home was well equipped to run a country. Not long before she fell publicly and tearfully out of office in 1990, she attended the annual Children of Courage service in Westminster Abbey. Dismayed at seeing a pile of unwrapped presents for the children, she demanded that brown paper and string be fetched. 'It's what we always used in the shop,' she said firmly – a pronouncement that would have been all too familiar to anyone who'd known her as she set up house in Swan Court over thirty years before.

Even during the rollercoaster of his eleven years as Downing Street consort, Denis kept his wry sense of humour about politics, once telling a stranger who wanted to know what his wife did that she had a temporary job. Asked who wore the trousers in Number 10, he replied, 'I do – and I wash and iron them as well'. Carol Thatcher admired the way her father always tried to diffuse difficult situations with humour – and a stiff drink. He lived on gin and cigarettes, she said, and made it to eighty-eight. Margaret Thatcher, inconsolable in widowhood, died at the same age in 2013, twenty-three years after leaving office.

MAIN SOURCES

Aitken, Jonathan: *Margaret Thatcher: Power and Personality*. Bloomsbury, 2013.

Cannadine, David: Essay on Denis Thatcher in *The Oxford Dictionary of National Biography*, January 4th 2007.

Cannadine, David: *Margaret Thatcher: A Life and Legacy*. Oxford University Press, 2017.

Moore, Charles: *Margaret Thatcher: The Authorised Biography*, Allen Lane, 2013-2019 Volume 1. *Not for Turning.*

Stothard, Peter: *The Senecans: Four Men and Margaret Thatcher*. Duckworth, 2016.

Thatcher, Carol: *Below the Parapet: The Biography of Denis Thatcher*. HarperCollins, 1996.

Thatcher, Margaret: *The Downing Street Years*. HarperCollins, 1993.

Thatcher, Margaret: *The Path to Power*. HarperCollins, 1995.

POSTSCRIPT
In Memoriam

Only four of this book's subjects lived to see the twenty-first century. With the death of Margaret Thatcher in 2013, all were gone but by no means forgotten; in the two decades since the millennium, many are still in the public eye. Sybil Thorndike, John Hayward, Virginia Cherrill, Naomi Royde-Smith, Agatha Christie and Margaret Thatcher have attracted biographers. Posthumous memoirs by Lesley Blanch and Rosalinde Fuller have appeared. Arthur Bryant and Dorothy Eckersley have found new notoriety as the subjects of academic analyses, and the lives of Anne Scott-James and Macdonald Hastings have been frankly recorded by their son. Francis Lorne's Wells Rise Terrace has figured in a book on Modernist architecture. A new edition of Edward McKnight Kauffer's biography came out in 2005, ten years before he and Marion Dorn were honoured with a blue plaque on the wall below their Swan Court studio. Marion Dorn's designs are prominent in refurbishments at Eltham Palace and the Art Deco Midland Hotel in Morecombe.

In 2012, when the BBC's World Service moved from Bush House to new quarters in Broadcasting House, several rooms were dedicated to past BBC giants. Despite the scandalous end to his BBC career, a room was named after Peter Eckersley to mark his major contribution as the Corporation's first Chief Engineer.

In 2014, for World Kindness Day, the British Film Institute asked people to nominate their favourite moments of kindness on film. Virginia Cherrill scooped the prize with her scene from *City Lights* where Charlie Chaplin's Tramp recognises the flower girl, a moment described as 'melting the heart'.

Agatha Christie's skills as a playwright are attracting new younger audiences with the production of *Witness for the Prosecution* – her favourite play – in the magnificent setting of the Council Chamber of City Hall on London's South Bank.

Now, in the spring of 2020, Peter Gregory's unfailing support of new talent is remembered once more as young poets submit their entries for this year's Gregory Poetry Awards. And in New York City, the Cooper-Hewitt Smithsonian Design Museum is preparing for a major exhibition of Edward McKnight Kauffer's work later in the year.

ACKNOWLEDGEMENTS

Among the people who have helped in the writing of this book, I am especially grateful to those family members who have so generously taken the time to talk to me about their forbears, loaned me books and helped with photographs and copyright. Particular thanks must go to Simon Rendall, Kenneth Saler Bruguière, Amanda Relph, Penny Pocock, Diana Devlin and Mathew Prichard. Thanks must also go to the late Sir Donald Sinden, the late Roger Morgan and Ellen Sheean for insights into the life and work of Ernest Milton.

I owe a debt to my neighbours Sarah Jackson and Peter Stewart, whose interest in Edward McKnight Kauffer and Marion Dorn and their time in Swan Court began it all. The invaluable London Library provided me with every book I needed as well as online access to journals and newspaper archives. My son Marcus Lyon and Joe Briggs-Price at The Glassworks gave unstinting professional help with the photographs. Special thanks must go to Jim Sutherland for the cover design and Rebecca Sutherland for the linocut of the two swans. I'm also very grateful to Don Grant for artistic insights, and to Anna Goddard, whose interest in an early draft encouraged me to persevere.

I am indebted to my husband Roger for his patience during the book's gestation, and deeply appreciative of his continuing interest in my subjects and his many helpful suggestions.

BIBLIOGRAPHY

Acton, Harold: *Memoirs of an Aesthete*. Methuen, 1948.
Aitken, Jonathan: *Margaret Thatcher: Power and Personality*. Bloomsbury, 2013.
Barker, Clive and Gale, Maggie B (eds): *British Theatre Between the Wars*. Cambridge University Press, 2000.
Barranger, Milly S: *Margaret Webster: A Life in the Theater*. University of Michigan Press, 2004.
Benton, Jill: *Avenging Muse: Naomi Royde-Smith 1875–1964*. Xlibris, 2015.
Blanch, Lesley: *Journey Into The Mind's Eye: Fragments of an Autobiography*. Collins, 1968.
Boston, Anne: *Lesley Blanch: Inner Landscapes, Wilder Shores*. John Murray, 2010.
Boydell, Christine: *The Architect of Floors: Modernism, Art and Marion Dorn Designs*. RIBA Heinz Gallery, 1996.
Boydell, Christine: 'The Decorative Imperative: Marion Dorn's Textiles and Modernism'. *The Journal of the Decorative Arts Society*, No.19, 1995.
Briggs, Asa: *The History of Broadcasting in the United Kingdom. Volumes I & II*. Oxford University Press, 1961.
Burke, David: *The Lawn Road Flats: Spies, Writers and Artists*. Boydell, 2014.
Cannadine, David: *Margaret Thatcher: A Life and Legacy*. Oxford University Press, 2017.
Casson, John: *Lewis and Sybil*. Collins, 1972.
Christie, Agatha: *An Autobiography*. Collins, 1977.
Christie, Agatha: *Come, Tell Me How You Live*. Collins, 1946.
Copsey, Nigel and Olechnowicz, Andrzej (eds): *Varieties of Anti-Fascism: Britain in the Inter-War Period*. Palgrave Macmillan, 2010.

Croall, Jonathan: *Sybil Thorndike: A Star of Life*. Haus Publishing, 2008.
Cullen, Stephen Michael: Strange Journey: The Life of Dorothy Eckersley. *The Historian*, Autumn 2013.
de Chamberet, Georgina: *On the Wilder Shores of Love: A Bohemian Life*. Virago, 2015.
de Courcy, Anne: *Diana Mosley*. Chatto & Windus, 2003.
Devlin, Diana: *A Speaking Part: Lewis Casson and the Theatre of his Time*. Hodder and Stoughton, 1982.
Diaper, Valerie: article about Eric Craven (Peter) Gregory in *The British Vision of World Art* by Herbert Read, Leeds City Art Galleries in association with the Henry Moore Foundation. Lund Humphries, 1993.
Ebert, Roger: *The Great Movies*. Broadway Books, 2002.
Eckersley, Miles: *Prospero's Wireless: PP Eckersley, A Biography*. Myles Books, 1997.
Enyeart, James: *Bruguière: His Photographs and his Life*. Alfred Knopf, 1987.
Gardner, Helen: *The Composition of Four Quartets*. Faber, 1978.
Gibbons Grinling, Antony: 'Wood as a Sculptural Material' in *Wood Magazine*, June 1936.
Gordon, Lyndall: *T.S. Eliot: An Imperfect Life*. WW Norton, 2000.
Gourvish, Terry: *Dolphin Square: The History of a Unique Building*. Bloomsbury, 2014.
Griffiths, Richard: *Fellow Travellers of the Right: British Enthusiasts for Nazi Germany 1933–1939*. Oxford University Press, 1983.
Griffiths, Richard: *What Did You Do During the War?: The Last Throes of the British pro-Nazi Right*. Routledge, 2017.
Guinness, Sir Alec: *Blessings in Disguise*. Hamish Hamilton, 1985.
Guinness, Bryan: *Dairy Not Kept*. Compton Press, 1975.
Guinness, Bryan: *Potpourri From the Thirties*. The Cygnet Press, 1982.
Guise, Barry and Brook, Pam: *The Midland Hotel: Morecombe's White Hope*. Palatine Books, 2007.
Harwood, Ronald: *Sir Donald Wolfit: His Life and Work in the Unfashionable Theatre*. Secker and Warburg, 1971.
Hastings, Max: *Did You Really Shoot the Television?: A Family Fable*. Harper Press, 2010.
Hattersley, Roy: *Borrowed Time: The Story of Britain Between the Wars*. Little Brown, 2007.
Haworth-Booth, Mark: *E. McKnight Kauffer: A Designer and his Public*.

V&A Publications, 2005.
Higgins, Charlotte: *This New Noise: The Extraordinary Birth and Troubled Life of the BBC*. Faber, 2015.
Holman, Valerie: *A Short History of Lund Humphries*. January 2014.
Huxley, Aldous: Introduction to Exhibition Catalogue, Museum of Modern Art, New York 1937.
Jensen, Finn: *Modernist Semis and Terraces in England*. Ashgate, 2012.
Keating, HRE (ed): *Agatha Christie: First Lady of Crime*. Weidenfeld and Nicolson, 1977.
Kenny, Mary: *Germany Calling: A Biography of William Joyce, Lord Haw-Haw*. Max Press, 2008.
Klaidman, Stephen: *Sydney and Violet: Their Life with T.S. Eliot, Proust, Joyce and the Excruciatingly Irascible Wyndham Lewis*. Doubleday, 2013.
Lancaster, Marie-Jaqueline (ed): *Brian Howard: Portrait of a Failure*. Blond, 1968.
Maland, Charles: *Chaplin and American Culture: The Evolution of a Star Image*. Princeton University Press, 1989.
Mallowan, Max: *Mallowan's Memoirs*. Collins, 1977.
Mallowan, Max: *Nimrud and its Remains*. Collins, 1966.
McIntyre, Ian: *The Expense of Glory: A life of John Reith*. HarperCollins, 1993.
Mellow, James R: *Invented Lives: F. Scott and Zelda Fitzgerald*. Souvenir Press, 1985.
Meynell, Francis: *My Lives*. Bodley Head, 1971.
Moore, Charles: *Margaret Thatcher: The Authorised Biography*. Allen Lane, 2013-2019 Vol.1 *Not for Turning*.
Morgan, Janet: *Agatha Christie: A Biography*. Collins, 1984.
Morley, Sheridan: *Sybil Thorndike: A Life in the Theatre*. Weidenfeld and Nicolson, 1977.
Morrison, Michael: *John Barrymore, Shakespearean Actor*. Cambridge University Press, 1997.
Mosley, Diana: *A Life*. Faber, 1999.
Mosley, Diana: *A Life of Contrasts*. Hamish Hamilton, 1977.
Murphy, Sean: *Letting the Side Down*. Sutton Publishing, 2003.
Northcote Parkinson, C: *A Law Unto Themselves*. John Murray, 1966.
Osborne, Charles: *The Life and Crimes of Agatha Christie*. Harper Collins, 1999.
Pevsner, Nicholas: 'Frank Pick'. In *Studies in Art, Architecture and Design*,

Vol. 2: *Victorian and After*. Thames & Hudson, 1968.
Powers, Alan: *Serge Chermayeff: Designer, Architect, Teacher*. RIBA, 2001.
Pugh, Martin: *We Danced All Night: A Social History of Britain Between the Wars*. Bodley Head, 2008.
Roberts, Andrew: *Eminent Churchillians*. Weidenfeld and Nicolson, 1994.
Robinson, W Sydney: *The Last Victorians*. The Robson Press, 2014.
Saler, Michael: *The Avant-Garde in Inter-War England: Medieval Modernism and the London Underground*. Oxford University Press, 2001.
Scannell, P and Cardiff, D: *A Social History of British Broadcasting. Vol. 1, 1922–1939: Serving the Nation*. Blackwell, 1991.
Scott-James, Anne: *In the Mink*. Michael Joseph, 1952.
Scott-James, Anne: *Sketches From a Life*. Michael Joseph, 1993.
Sekules, Veronica: 'The Ship-Owner as an Art Patron: Sir Colin Anderson and the Orient Line 1930–1960'. *The Journal of The Decorative Arts Society*, 1986.
Seymour, Miranda: *Chaplin's Girl: The Life and Loves of Virginia Cherrill*. Simon and Schuster, 2009.
Skipwith, Peyton: *Sculpture in Britain Between the Wars*. Fine Art Society, 1986.
Smart, John: *Tarantula's Web: John Hayward, TS Eliot and Their Circle*. Michael Russell Ltd, 2013.
Smith, Emma: *As Green as Grass*. Bloomsbury, 2013.
Sprigge, Elizabeth: *Sybil Thorndike Casson*. Victor Gollancz, 1971.
Stothard, Peter: *The Senecans: Four Men and Margaret Thatcher*. Duckworth, 2016.
Street, Pamela: *Arthur Bryant: Portrait of a Historian*. Collins, 1979.
Stuart, Charles (ed): *The Reith Diaries*. Collins, 1975.
Taylor, DJ: *Bright Young People: The Rise and Fall of a Generation 1918–1940*. Vintage, 2008.
Thatcher, Carol: *Below the Parapet: The Biography of Denis Thatcher*. HarperCollins, 1996.
Thatcher, Margaret: *The Downing Street Years*. HarperCollins, 1993.
Thatcher, Margaret: *The Path to Power*. HarperCollins, 1995.
Thompson, Laura: *Agatha Christie: An English Mystery*. Headline Review, 2007.
Todd, D: 'Marion Dorn: Architect of Floors'. In *Architectural Review*, 72, 1932.
Vincent, GK: *A History of Du Cane Court: Land, Architecture, People and

Politics. Fastprint Publishing, 2013.

Waugh, Alec: *Thirteen Such Years*. Cassell, 1932.

Webb, Brian and Skipwith, Peyton: *Design: E. McKnight Kauffer*. Antique Collectors' Club, 2007.

Wheal, Donald James: *World's End: A Memoir of a Blitz Childhood*. Century, 2005.

Whistler, Theresa: *The Imagination of the Heart: The Life of Walter de la Mare*. Duckworth, 1993.

Winnington, Peter G (ed): *Kissing the Joy: The Autobiography of Rosalinde Fuller OBE*. Letterworth Press (e-book), 2018.

Winnington, Peter G: *Walter Fuller: The Man Who Had Ideas*. Letterworth Press, 2014.

Woolf, Virginia: *Diaries*. Hogarth Press, 1978.

Wyndham, Joan: *Love Lessons: A Wartime Diary*. Heineman, 1985.

Wyndham, Lewis: '*Modernism*' in The Architectural Review, November 1934.